Advance Praise for What Every Kid Needs
—and Money Can't Buy

"Keith's book and his live presentations move audiences to tears of laughter, self-identification, and empathy … often in the same story and sometimes in the same sentence. But what Keith does best is motivate people to action."

—FRED KEATING, ACTOR, WRITER,
MOTIVATIONAL SPEAKER

"Keith is a dream weaver whose words have changed the lives of children in untold ways.… Once [young people] learn to believe, there is nothing that can hold them back from reaching for the stars. This book may just be the star field of hopes that every kid needs."

—PATSY GEORGE, CM, OBC, LLD (HON)

"Keith embodies the quintessential educator. He believes strongly in what he is doing and is able to transmit this to his audiences in a very effective manner. What more can I say?"

—FRAN GRUNBERG, FACULTY, SOCIAL SERVICE
WORKER PROGRAM, LANGARA COLLEGE

"Keith's message of asset building, presented through the eyes of a consummate storyteller, gives those new to asset building an opportunity to say 'I can do this.'"

—CATHY CROSS, COMMUNITY
SCHOOL COORDINATOR

"*I have witnessed the magic of being deliberate and intentional in our positive interactions with young people in communities … and the difference it makes. Our kids need to be inspired and empowered to make a difference, and the stories Keith shares are a great place to start!*"

—PATRICIA HOWELL-BLACKMORE, DIRECTOR
OF COMMUNICATIONS AND PROGRAMS,
LIONS QUEST CANADA—THE CANADIAN CENTRE
FOR POSITIVE YOUTH DEVELOPMENT

"*Keith's heart-warming, funny, poignant, and all too often so-close-to-home stories are priceless. He has the ability to convey what we need to do to create a better world for our kids in a magical way.… Two thumbs up!*"

—JAMES VOLLBRACHT, EDUCATOR, SPEAKER,
AND AUTHOR OF, AMONG OTHER TITLES,
How to Create a Culture that Cares for Kids

"*Keith shares stories about making connections and building relationships for a fleeting moment at the checkout line, helping to build a relationship with our kids and others. It's about planting seeds in people—one smile, one person, or one starfish at a time. Cost: priceless.*"

—DARLENE JAMIESON, PARENT, COMMUNITY
MEMBER, SOCIAL JUSTICE WORKER, SEED PLANTER

What Every Kid Needs
—and Money Can't Buy

What Every Kid Needs
—and Money Can't Buy

Ideas and stories to
help you make a difference

KEITH PATTINSON

Keith Pattinson & Friends
www.keithpattinson.com
kpattinson@dccnet.com

The 40 Developmental Assets framework, lists, charts, handouts, data, and statistics included in this publication have been reprinted with permission from Search Institute, 615 First Avenue NE, Suite 125, Minneapolis, MN 55413. All rights reserved. To learn more about the Developmental Assets or Search Institute, please visit www.search-institute.org.

The following are registered trademarks of Search Institute: Search Institute™, Developmental Assets™, Health Communities • Healthy Youth™, and Parent-Further™.

Layout and design: Jan Westendorp, Kato Design & Photo
Editing and proofreading: Naomi Pauls, Paper Trail Publishing
Indexing: Bookmark: Editing & Indexing

Cover photo: Jan Westendorp, Kato Design & Photo
Author photo on back cover: Michael Moster, Michael's Fine Photography

Library and Archives Canada Cataloguing in Publication

Pattinson, Keith
    What every kid needs—and money can't buy : ideas and stories to help you make a difference / Keith Pattinson.

Includes bibliographical references and index.
ISBN 978-0-9917132-0-2

    1. Child development. 2. Children—Counseling of.
3. Youth—Counseling of. 4. Children and adults.
5. Mentoring. 6. Parenting. I. Title.

HQ767.9.P38 2012   649'.6   C2012-907330-X

Typeset in Whitman, Optima, and URW Grotesk

Printed in Victoria, B.C., by Printorium Bookworks, a division of Island Blue Print Co. Ltd., on 100% recycled paper

To my wife and best friend, Maureen,
our children, and our grandchildren,
who together have taught me more
life lessons than any class I ever
attended or book I ever opened.

Contents

Foreword

I CONSIDER MYSELF EXTREMELY fortunate to have crossed paths with Keith Pattinson. His work has allowed me to appreciate the importance of making a difference in a young person's life. Keith has played an instrumental role in opening my eyes to the benefits of applying a strength-based approach both as a police officer and as a parent.

As a detachment commander, I have seen how the lives of young people can be positively affected when a community dares to start catching their kids doing something right. The Asset Approach empowers police officers and all adults alike with the tools to change young people's lives on a daily basis. The most rewarding and successful policing initiatives I have implemented have come from focusing on what matters to the vast majority of our kids, rather than solely on what's the matter with a small minority of kids.

Apart from my police work, Keith Pattinson's words and actions have inspired me as a parent to consciously and intentionally apply positive principles and approaches in raising my two teenage children. Our actions as parents are guided not by what we can afford to do, but rather by what actions we take to ensure that our children have the necessary building blocks to succeed in life. Most of these actions cost us only our time.

Our family recently moved in the middle of the school year, resulting in our son, who was in Grade 10, attending his seventh school. Such constant moves can be hard on kids. Yet evidence of the positive impact of the Asset Approach is overwhelming. Both our teenagers are consistent honour students, maintain a strong ability to cope with a changing environment, and have a diverse and healthy group of friends—and they still like to do things with Mom and Dad!

As a senior police officer and a father, I am often reminded of Keith's oft-quoted declaration that asset development is above all about relationships, personal involvement, and the courage to act. In both my role as a father and in the work I have been able to do with young people as a detachment commander, his ideas, stories, and approach have played a critical role in my success. They have enabled me to present credible solutions to chronic youth issues where before no effective solutions were provided—just programs. They have enabled me to successfully obtain resources necessary to address important youth issues and offer community-wide approaches to policing challenges, instead of futilely trying to deal with them as a "police" issue. I recommend this book to anyone who wants to help kids succeed.

—Supt. Warren Dosko
officer in charge, Red Deer
Detachment, rcmp

Preface

"WHY DON'T YOU WRITE A BOOK, KEITH?" For the past fifteen or twenty years, I have heard that recurring refrain from audiences—most often moms and dads intent on being the best parents they can possibly be. And they know what they want and don't want in this book they have asked me to write. They don't want to be judged, blamed, or faulted for making the kinds of innocent mistakes most of us do when we take on the most complex venture of our lives—the raising of healthy children and young people. And they don't want a bunch of complex theories that are hard to understand and even harder to implement.

They have told me over and over again that they want practical ideas they can apply every day. The 40 Developmental Assets approach of Search Institute in Minneapolis has worked for or intrigues many of them, and they want a straightforward guide to this strength-based approach so they can better help all kids achieve their potential. They seek successful strategies used by other parents, and above all they want stories and more stories that give them hope and help them envision how success in raising healthy and happy kids looks and feels. This book is my response to their ideas and requests. Here's what I hope you will get out of it.

As a parent or significant other in the life of a child, you may gain confidence and discover you are doing a better job than you thought you were. Many of the things you have done intuitively, you will find are far more important than you thought they were and deserve more attention. They are things you are already doing, and you may conclude they deserve more emphasis. You will be reminded that what you say to children is important, but how you behave in their presence will have the greatest impact. You will learn that the values, experiences, and stories you share casually with children can be life-changing and are therefore worth sharing more often and more intentionally.

Above all, you may finish reading this book more committed to acting upon an old First Nations saying: "What we want from our children … we must first give them." Although parents are my first and primary audience, this book is also written for many other people in children's lives. It is meant for grandparents, educators, youth workers, police officers, neighbours, young people, and anyone else who believes that what we as individuals invest in our kids' lives will eventually come back into our own. It's a book about what we can all offer children to better assure their success in life.

I have heard it said that in times of change, it will be the *learners* among us who will inherit the earth, while the *learned* will carry on being equipped to deal only with a world that no longer exists. This book comes from a lifelong learner, a less-than-perfect father, grandfather, and fellow traveller in this remarkable adventure we share in raising healthy, responsible children. It offers compelling evidence that the care, nurturing, and respect young people receive from the significant people in their lives makes them more respectful, compassionate, and productive.

You may come to share my belief that young people need three important things in order to achieve their potential in life. The three things are relationships, relationships, and relationships. For the children in your life, what is important is not how big a house you live in, how impressive a car you drive, or how much money you have in your bank account. Rather, relationships are our most important legacy. This book explores the opportunity each of us has every day to develop significant relationships in the lives of the children and young people who are, or who could be, within our influence.

Many years ago, I attended a gang prevention conference in Atlanta, Georgia. Organizers had invited four of the city's most renowned gang recruiters to talk of their successes. These kids ranged in age from fourteen to nineteen. At the conclusion of their compelling description of gang life and recruiting methods, they opened the floor for questions. A man who described himself as the CEO of a major youth organization asked the question that was on many minds that day. "What is it that you know and do that seems to make you so much more successful at attracting teen members than many of us?"

The youngest recruiter, a fourteen-year-old boy, gave the answer that to this day strikes fear in my heart. "Mister, we've learned how to respect 'em, involve 'em, and love 'em better than you do!"

This book is about how you and I can respect, involve, and love young people better than gangs do! At the risk of being overly dramatic, I believe the future of our kids and maybe our society depends on our willingness and capacity to respond to this challenge. Together, we can and will assure our young people the future they deserve and that humankind so desperately needs.

———

A few short "housekeeping announcements" before we begin:

Quotations: To the extent possible, I have attempted to source and credit each of the quotes sprinkled throughout the book. In the case of any errors or omissions, I would be pleased to make corrections in future editions.

Stories: Sourcing informal and at times apocryphal tales was a bigger challenge. Wherever possible, I have given appropriate credit. Exceptions include stories that seemed indistinguishable from urban legend—heard and told countless times over the years, with a seemingly endless number of versions. For these I have offered my best attempt at an accurate rendition, recognizing that these stories may appear to some to be a figment of my imagination.

Statistics: Every effort has been made to credit and reproduce statistics, graphs, and charts in a form and format consistent with the wishes of those who granted permission for their inclusion in this book. Any errors, omissions, or obfuscations are mine and only mine.

Developmental Assets: The list of 40 Developmental Assets in chapter 5 is used with permission from Search Institute, 700 South Third Street, Suite 210, Minneapolis, MN 55415, www.Search-Institute.org. Additional material in this book was originally published by Search Institute and has been reprinted with permission. For a full list of permissions, please consult page 154.

Acknowledgements

THIS BOOK IS DEDICATED to two friends who have made a profound difference in my life. The first is the late Brian R. Sawyer, 1930–2012, former RCMP superintendent, Chief of the Calgary Police Service, vice-president of Canadian Airlines, and former Provincial Ombudsman, Province of Alberta, who taught me forty years ago that police officers could and would change the world for the better for all children, youth, and their families.

I also dedicate this book to William J. "Bill" Snowdon, retired chief, Victoria Police Department, past vice-president, Canadian Association of Chiefs of Police, member of the National Parole Board, and president of Boys and Girls Clubs of Canada. Besides being a friend, Bill is a police leader, extraordinary volunteer, and role model whose professional/volunteer career has centred on service to others. To this day a "catcher of kids doing something right," Bill never fails to stop at every kid's lemonade stand he encounters.

This book is also written in memory of Peter Lorimer Benson, former president/CEO of Search Institute of Minneapolis, a.k.a. "Mr. Helping Kids Succeed." He was the first person to introduce the 40 Developmental Assets into my life. Peter's vision has inspired over 600 community-based initiatives in 45 states, every Canadian province, and on six continents. He was an international leader in teaching parents and communities how to help children achieve their potential.

Many others also deserve my deepest gratitude. My parents, Joseph and May Pattinson, taught me by example that material things are not the essence of life, that service is the rent we pay for the space we occupy on earth. Thanks also to my sister, Elizabeth Ann Carviel, a compassionate nurse, awesome friend, and champion in my life.

In the field of youth development, all of the following have earned my heartfelt gratitude for the work they do. My colleague Ward Clapham helped pioneer and continues to champion the asset-building idea throughout the world. Barry King, retired Chief of Ontario's Brockville Police Service helped to bring the Canadian Association of Chiefs of Police onside in support of training and encouraging police officers across Canada to focus on the desire of most kids to be part of the solution, not the problem. Larry Thomas, former superintendent, Skaha School District 67, introduced education-based asset-building approaches in the Penticton/Summerland school system in 1998, for the first time in Canada, and played a key role in advancing the approach in Boys and Girls Clubs and voluntary agencies throughout British Columbia. Jo-Anne Lauzer, M.Ed., is a talented counsellor, friend, and mentor without whose patience, encouragement, and media savvy this book would never have been written. My thanks to RCMP Supt. Warren Dosko, a four-community veteran of asset building—no doubt with more to come. I also acknowledge Ralph Hembruff, Boys and Girls Clubs of Canada; Rhonda Brown, Big Brothers/Big Sisters of Victoria; Joanne McQuiggan and Pat Howell-Blackmore of Lions Quest Canada, pioneers in the Canadian asset-building community; Tim and Donna Duffey and the Vision Training Trainers who carry Search Institute's asset-building message throughout the world; and Robert M. Moffat, trial lawyer, volunteer exemplar, and priceless friend.

Writing a book and the whole business of self-publishing was a new adventure, and I relied on the support of my wife and family members throughout the process. I also appreciate the encouragement and assistance I received from publishing professionals. I thank my editor, Naomi Pauls of Paper Trail Publishing, whose magic way with words and phrases showed me that effective editing offers the most priceless advantage an author can ask for. Likewise, I acknowledge Jan Westendorp of Kato Design & Photo, the miracle worker behind this book's cover and interior design.

My thanks to thirteen-year-old Willem, the teen behind the cover profile. We couldn't have done it without you, Willem!

My appreciation goes out to the many people whose names and experiences appear in these pages and who have kindly risked their considerable reputations by allowing me to share their story.

Finally, and most importantly, I acknowledge the thousands of young people throughout the world who every day offer their time, talent, wisdom, and energy as they join forces with significant adults in their lives to build a better environment in which we all may live in peace, respect, and safety.

Chapter 1

The Magic of
Significant People

One hundred years from now,... the world may be a little
better because I was important in the life of a child.
—FOREST WITCRAFT, "Within My Power"

MY BFO (BLINDING FLASH OF THE OBVIOUS) occurred in the early 1950s. I was in Grade 12, my final year of high school in Kamloops, British Columbia, and it went down something like this. I was an academically average student, forgettable basketball player, president of the combined junior/senior student council. In November of that senior year I had maybe a little too much time on my hands, having just abandoned the chance to travel to Europe as a member of our high school band. My ambition? To finish high school. Not bad . . . but not great.

Enter into my day one large, blunt, and sometimes menacing presence in the person of my physical education teacher, Mr. Nick Turik. I received a "summons to appear" before him in his office in the basement adjacent to the school gym, never an invitation to be taken lightly. Our meeting began with me sitting-in-wait in his office, looking and feeling somewhat diminished, another victim of his legendary "glower."

"You sent for me, Mr. Turik?"

"I didn't think I'd ever hear myself saying this, Pattinson, but I need your help."

"You've got to be kidding!" came out of my mouth before I could catch myself.

"I wish I was, but no. Here's the deal. The coach of the junior boys basketball team has transferred to another school in mid-season. I'm asking you to coach the team."

I could not conceal my surprise at this request. "Mr. Turik, I don't know anything about coaching basketball," I said.

"Tell me something I don't know, Pattinson. But have you forgotten you attend a school where every day you get to watch me in action as a coach?"

In a quieter and less convincing voice I recall answering, "Of course, sir, I'd completely forgotten about that. But anyway, I'm pretty busy right now."

Looking displeased but unrelenting, Coach continued, "Too busy, eh? Got better things to do? That's too bad. Well, you should at least know why I'm even asking you. You see, I met with the kids on the team a couple of days ago and asked them to get together and put down the name of someone they'd like to have as a coach. Didn't think I had a democratic side, did you, Pattinson? They all put down your name. Just goes to show what *they* know. Now, I've got to meet them tonight and tell them *why you said no.*" He paused to make sure his words were getting through.

"So you owe me a small favour, Pattinson," continued Mr. Turik, narrowing his eyes and leaning back in his chair. "Tell me what you want me to say to those kids tonight."

I looked down at the floor, wiped my sweaty palms on my jeans, and wracked my brain for a way out of my corner. After a lot of uncomfortable fidgeting in a fifteen-second silence that felt like an hour, I offered a hesitant and perhaps desperation-driven response. "Okay, Mr. Turik," I said. "I'll do it!"

With that the perpetually scowling Nick Turik unfolded his substantial physique from behind his desk, walked in my direction, gave me one of his best eye-to-eye stares, and put eight words together in a single sentence. "Thanks, Keith, you're going to make a difference!" I left his office unsure whether to take his comment as a prediction, a threat, or a promise.

To this day, I am still not sure if I made any difference in the lives of the ten kids on that team so many years ago, but after five months of coaching them, I knew those kids had changed my life forever. We won a few games and lost more than our share, but in the end it was the journey, not the final standings that really mattered. A ragtag bunch of kids and a guy the age of an older brother ended the season having gained confidence that only comes to those prepared to give more than they get out of sports and life.

And yes, there is a "rest of the story" about my high school coach. In the spring of 2011, I found that same Nick Turik I had not seen for nearly sixty years and could not resist his invitation to drop in for a visit. "I'm writing a book about significant people in kids' lives, Nick, and I need your help," I said. "I'm asking you to read these few pages. With your permission, I'd like to use them at the beginning of my book."

Coach Turik took the time to read the story carefully and respond. "I like it, Keith. You're going to make a difference!" At that moment—and for the first time in my life—I understood it was a prediction he had given me in his office that day so long ago, for that was when my lifetime of working with kids and families really began.

"They made a difference in my life." This is a sentiment people often express when reflecting on someone who was there when they needed them most. For many of us, relationships with significant people during our formative years help to determine our beliefs, values, and behaviours. Of course, children first and foremost need adequate health care, shelter, food, clothing, education, and other basic necessities of life. That is a given. But when most of us engage in a life self-review to determine our behavioural roots, chances are good that rather than focus on the material things we were given, we will focus on the time shared with us by others.

Most of us naturally develop close relationships with our own children and younger relations. However, it has never been easy to take that first step toward becoming an enduring significant influence in the lives of young people outside our family circle. Yet doing so, I would argue, is neither new-fangled nor complicated: simply take the time to learn and remember their names. Look for an opportunity to find out what is important in their life as a young person who may need and want your interest, time, support, and encouragement. Maybe your chat is about their favourite sport, special friend, best or worst subject in school, or athletic achievement. Then, the next time you meet, ask a question or make a comment that confirms to them you cared enough to remember what they told you.

It might help to take a quick look at this notion of significant people. Where do they come from? What do they look like? Who trains them and what defines "significant"? I am a great believer in the power of personal stories to convey important ideas. What follows is an account of one of my briefest yet most memorable encounters as a youth with "significant others." This experience shows how two neighbours changed my life in a matter of minutes.

I grew up in the then small town of Kamloops in British Columbia's interior, and it was here on a bright and sunny spring day that I learned one of life's most important lessons. The lesson came not from my parents or teachers but from a couple of neighbours who understood the values instilled in me by my parents and who took the time to remind me of them.

In 1946 I was ten years old and in Grade 4 at the Lloyd George Elementary School, where my teacher was Mrs. Nixon. On this particular Thursday morning in May, fishing, not attending school, was the highest of my priorities. I had been reading *Field and Stream* magazine and the even more authoritative *Kamloops Sentinel* and had reached the conclusion that the reason for my failure to be published and honoured as a world-class fisherman rested almost certainly upon the fact that my fishing expeditions were restricted to weekends. During the week, in contrast, fishing pressure on the nearby Thompson River was markedly lower. With that in mind, I had decided to skip school for the first time. This was not a decision taken lightly, as my parents had made it clear they valued education and so should I. However, I had concluded that once they saw my published colour photo with a record Kamloops trout in *Field and Stream* magazine, all school skipping transgressions would be forgiven.

As was customary, my parents left for work early that spring morning. I lingered behind until my sister finally headed for classes at a nearby junior high school. Once she had left, I made my move to the basement, where I pocketed a fishing line and hook, wrapped discreetly around a piece of wood, slipped some bait in the other pocket, and headed out to walk the few blocks north to the Thompson River and the awaiting trophy fish.

I had travelled only two houses away from my front door when I was greeted by an elderly neighbour whom I knew as a pensioner, someone who always said "Hi Keith" as I walked by. After his customary "How are you doing?" he followed with the somewhat assertive question: "Are you lost?" I responded lamely, "No, just checking out a new paper route," to which he replied, "Have a good day in school, Keith."

The encounter shook my confidence slightly, but the fish continued to have more appeal than Grade 4 and Mrs. Nixon, so I carried on. Another neighbour a couple of houses farther along was leaning over her front fence pruning her roses. I knew Mrs. Simpson, an eighty-year-old widow, because I spent time cutting her lawn in the summer and shovelling snow from her walks in the winter. My dad thought I had some kind of benevolent streak, but the truth was she made the best hot chocolate and cookies in all of Kamloops. We would sometimes sit for hours around her old wood stove while she listened patiently to my adventures and then regaled me with stories of her life and her travels around the world.

On this Thursday school morning she looked up as I went by and inquired, "Hi Keith. Will you be able to come and cut my lawn after school today?" I remember impishly telling her that I would be there for sure, maybe even a bit early, to which she quietly responded, "That's good, Keith, because you've always been so honest and trustworthy."

And it was at that moment that my fishing trip came to an abrupt end. This happened without the intervention of a school truancy officer, teachers, or parents—without even a lecture. It was a neighbour who set me right—a neighbour who knew enough about me and my family and who cared enough to take the time to get me back on track. I did not skip school again (at least not throughout elementary school), because every time I even thought about it, Mrs. Simpson's words would come back to haunt me. "Keith, you've always been so honest and trustworthy."

As I travel, speaking to communities throughout North America, I am saddened to see growing evidence that many neighbours no longer greet one another by name. In fact, many times they do not even know who their neighbours are. As a result, parents and their children are being deprived of this priceless network of caring adults who throughout history have so effectively shared in the raising of healthy, happy, and responsible young people.

This is one of the reasons we need to find safe ways to reduce the number of "strangers" in our children's lives and intentionally connect them with appropriate role models: people we know and trust, people we feel could and should become significant in our children's lives. The next chapter presents a six-minute exercise I have shared with thousands of workshop participants intent on understanding this majestic notion of significant people and, more importantly, knowing how they can *become* one.

LESSONS TO TAKE AWAY

1. Most children and young people today lack a strong network of caring adults who function as appropriate role models.

2. By taking time to demonstrate an intentional interest in the lives of individual children, each of us can become significant in children's lives every day.

3. Even small acts and simple words can have a lasting positive impression on the young. It's up to us to make the conscious effort!

Chapter 2

Who Was There
for You?

He ain't heavy, Father ... he's m'brother!
—WORDS ON A STATUE OF A BOY CARRYING
A SMALLER BOY ON HIS BACK, SYMBOLIZING
THE WORK OF BOYS TOWN, NEBRASKA

To FULLY UNDERSTAND THE CONCEPT of significant people, it is helpful to look back at our own lives and remember
adults who influenced us when we were young. Perhaps a certain
teacher instilled confidence and pride. That person could be a
relative, a coach, or a member of your congregation. What did
they help you learn about yourself and others that assisted you on
your life path?

Depending on your life experience, you may have already
thought about these mentors and made these important personal
discoveries. In this case, the brief exercise presented in this chapter may simply refocus or reaffirm the foundation upon which
you can begin to become more intentional in your mentoring
relationships with children and youth. Experience tells me there
is a good chance that you will walk away with a new or enhanced
understanding of some of the important values you hold. It can

be fun and reaffirming to share your findings with a friend, colleague, or partner, whether now or later.

Here is the three-step exercise many have found vital in helping them understand this notion of significant people, the important role they play, and how they themselves can become significant in the lives of others.

Step 1. Remember a significant person

Start by taking a quiet minute to look back on your own childhood, sometime between the ages of six and eighteen years. Reflect on your growing years and focus on one person who was an important influence in your life. Many of you will be lucky. You will be reminded of many such people and the legacy they have left in your life.

Be forewarned that through reflection you could identify a significant *negative* experience that changed your life. One workshop participant told me: "As a young kid I lived next door to an abusive alcoholic and watched and listened to how he treated his children and family. I decided I never wanted to grow up to be like him." This comment reminds us that young people have a remarkable capacity to take a seemingly negative experience and turn it into something constructive in their lives. For most of you, though, the experiences will be positive—and remember, there is no pass or fail with this exercise.

Step 2. Describe what made them significant

With the image of that one significant person in mind, describe in several sentences what makes them so memorable and important in your life. Place the name of your chosen significant person at the top of a blank page and then list the important qualities or approaches or whatever you recall they brought to your relationship. If it helps, begin with words that describe their character. You'll recall I began this book by sharing my reflections of Nick Turik, a teacher and basketball coach whose qualities and approach I can recall, describe, and often emulate to this day.

Step 3. Share your findings with another person

When I present this exercise in a group setting, at this point people share their findings one-on-one with another participant. They are asked to talk about their "significant other" (in three minutes or less) and describe what made that individual such an important and often life-changing influence. As you wrap up the exercise with a partner—or tell a young person you know!—I hope you will have reminded yourself of the influence and legacy of the significant person in your life.

As I said, thousands of others have completed this exercise in workshop settings. Here is a sampling of their responses and observations so you can compare your reflections with what other participants have told me.

"In three minutes? You've got to be kidding" is one of the most common responses I have heard. And in reality, this three-minute rule seldom works. Sometimes it is almost impossible to get total strangers to *stop* talking and sharing about a topic few have had the encouragement or previous opportunity to talk and think about. Responses are often profound and always instructive. For many, this short exercise represents a unique opportunity to reflect on important life experiences and be reminded of practical ideas they can use every day to improve the way they relate to young people.

What significant people did they talk about? The list is a long one: moms, dads, neighbours, coaches, teachers, friends, aunts, uncles, grandparents, ministers, employers, nephews, nieces, and remarkably, in one instance, a total stranger. Significant people who have influenced children and youth come from all walks of life, and with few exceptions they made their influence felt at a cost of nothing more than the time it took.

What made these people significant? Here are the comments I have heard most frequently:

- They took the time to listen as if what I had to say was important.

- They taught me by example.

- They were positive and honest.

- While they didn't always like what I did, they always liked me.

- They were caring and supportive.

- They were enthusiastic.

- When I was wrong they told me and then helped me to make a better choice.

- They were giving.

- They encouraged and helped me when I was discouraged.

- They focused on my strengths and helped me to see and achieve my potential.

- They were reliable and trustworthy.

- They always showed they liked and respected me.

Does that sound like somebody you would have liked to be around when you were a kid? More importantly, does it sound like someone you are or would like to become? If your answer is yes, let's get started now by defining and developing this priceless opportunity that exists for each of us.

Begin by reflecting on just a couple of points drawn from the true story of my aborted fishing expedition in chapter 1. How did Mrs. Simpson, an eighty-year-old widow, manage to change my life forever in the space of less than a minute? Each of you has the capacity to find that minute and to make that irreplaceable difference.

She took the time to know my name, to gain the trust and respect of my family, and to learn something of our values and expectations. She always treated me and every kid on our block with respect, and that respect, I recall, was in turn bestowed upon her through every interaction we had with her. I now appreciate how profound was her understanding of a kid's real needs. You see, she knew the fifty cents she paid me to cut her lawn or shovel her sidewalk gave me a reason to spend hours volunteering in her amazing garden, from where I took home to my family an endless supply of fresh vegetables. It also gave me an unlimited opportunity to sit, sometimes for hours, to listen to her stories and, more importantly, to have her patiently listen to mine.

Becoming significant is not necessarily about finding more time in what is for many of us an already inordinately hectic schedule. Mrs. Simpson became significant by simply prioritizing how she spent the time she had: in the fishing story, she spent only a few seconds redirecting a transgressing ten-year-old boy.

The Issue of Safety

With very good reasons, the safety factor is bound to be raised when adults are encouraged to expand their healthy interest and influence in young people's lives. Security should be foremost in the mind of every adult responsible for the safe passage of children through life. One of the best summations in response to the challenge of assuring child safety came at one of many workshops I have conducted for police officers throughout Canada. We were discussing how to build enhanced and respectful adult-youth relationships as a means to help make our streets and neighbourhood safer and more welcoming for young people.

A veteran police officer spoke up: "Keith, here's how I see it. Statistically we know that about 3 percent of the adult population should be nowhere near young people, but the problem is that in the process of trying to protect our kids from the 3 percent, we have unintentionally disconnected them from the roughly 97 percent, many of whom hold potential to change the lives of kids for the better every day."

Trusted neighbours, grandparents, relatives, friends, and senior citizens could all play an important expanded role in the everyday lives of children. This is both desirable and possible when safety concerns are thoughtfully identified, challenged, and addressed.

In light of these legitimate safety concerns and lost possibilities, my best advice is to first and foremost honour and act on your own perception of whatever is safe, based on your own life experience and that of the children within your influence. Continue to seek out new relational opportunities you can comfortably introduce to assure young people are not denied the influence of their "village," the mentoring, teaching, and role modelling experiences generations of Canadians have identified as critically important to their healthy development.

Here are some practical steps you can begin taking to become more connected to and influential in the lives of young people.

- *Address children directly.* Learn the names of children and youth in your neighbourhood, apartment complex, or place of work. Speak to them by name, kneel down and look them in the eye if they are small, and above all show a real interest in and remember what they have to say.

- *Invite friends along.* If you are a champion of family outings and events, consider having your children invite one or two friends along, maybe youngsters who have limited opportunity to participate in the kinds of activities you enjoy. You will telegraph the message that you trust your children's judgement and signal to other parents that it is possible to safely broaden our kids' life experiences. An unanticipated benefit is that both parents and kids are inclined to behave better in such a group. And wouldn't every parent appreciate shared responsibility in preventing the boredom that kids on their own are prone to exhibit?

- *Engage with young people.* Take the time to learn the names of young people who work as cashiers at your local supermarket or pack your groceries. Ask them how they are doing at school, in sports, or in life. You may be pleasantly surprised at their response to someone showing real interest. Tell them how you admire them working part-time as well as pursuing their education. Remember to follow up next time you shop, and ask them how their sick pet is doing or how they did on the math exam they were worried about.

- *Break down barriers.* When you pass teenagers—including those resplendent in multiple piercings, hoodies, and half-mast jeans—while you are walking the dog, shopping in a mall, sitting on a transit bus, or lining up at a cash register, take a couple of seconds to establish eye contact. This will not always be reciprocated on the first attempt. Greet them with a friendly "Hi there" or "Hello." Like the adults in their lives, some will respond and others won't . . . but frequently you will find that such a simple act will reinforce evidence of your interest and friendliness. Making the initial effort also shows kids that many of us adults recognize we have some responsibility to break down the communication barriers if we expect kids to be more engaged with us.

- *Take a teen along.* If you volunteer within your community, check out the possibility of taking a young volunteer assistant with you. Many kids today are unaware of the notion of community service, not because they do not care, but because they have not been shown the possibilities. What better way to introduce young people to the rewards and satisfactions of volunteering than by giving them a real opportunity to sense and gain the positive recognition that comes from doing something for someone else?

A major theme of this book is that "becoming significant" is something within your control. It is about the personal time you and I spend or do not spend encouraging, influencing, and supporting children. But before we delve more into the "how," let's have a quick look at the current state of the world—social realities that make the need for mentoring of young people even more urgent.

LESSONS TO TAKE AWAY

1. When we were growing up, we all had "significant people" who influenced our lives in important ways.

2. Identifying our own mentors and the things they taught us can help us recognize our own key values and our sometimes forgotten capacity to make a difference in children's lives.

3. By recognizing the simple ways these mentors influenced us, sometimes by merely "spending time," we can see ways we too can connect with and influence young people.

Chapter 3

The How-to of
Becoming Significant

*It's about relationships. When you build
relationships, you build trust ... and when
you have trust, anything can happen.*
—WAYNE YEE, ADVISOR, YOUTH SERVICES,
CITY OF RICHMOND, B.C.

To BRING ABOUT SUCCESS for all children, we need to face
the facts: society's current response to the social ills facing
children, youth, and families is in disarray. Every day, the media
remind us that as a functioning society we are in retreat. After
decades of launching "wars" on violence, drugs, poverty, family
breakdown, and illiteracy, we continue to experience these in
abundance, and they are having a devastating impact on children
and families.

As if that is not discouraging enough, we also seem to be running out of the ideas, energy, and sound leadership necessary to
achieve success in any war. Our situation is somewhat akin to
that of the World War I Canadian pilot whose aircraft plummeted
to earth, leaving him the inglorious task of explaining the circumstances in writing to his superior officer. In response to the

question "What caused your plane to crash?" he wrote, "I ran out of airspeed, altitude, and ideas, simultaneously."

To continue the military metaphor, the bad news is that in our battle to bring about social reform, we are running out of airspeed, altitude, and ideas at an alarming rate, particularly as it affects our young people. But there is also good news: a relatively new idea supported by evidence that it can help to counter those wrongs and has everything to do with what is, or could be, going right in communities. Healthy Communities • Healthy Youth is the result of over forty years of research and work by Search Institute of Minneapolis, Minnesota. Originating in 1958 as the Lutheran Youth Research Center, Search Institute is a nonprofit organization with worldwide influence bringing, in its own words, "hopeful solutions to pressing challenges in the lives of young people and their communities."

In the chapters to follow, you will find information about Search Institute's 40 Developmental Assets, described as "the positive relationships, opportunities, competencies, values, and self-perceptions youth need to succeed." You may choose to think of them as forty life "building blocks" that you can easily understand, then introduce and enhance in the lives of children within your influence.

Of equal or even greater importance, you will learn of Search Institute's research-based findings that offer compelling evidence that the presence of these Developmental Assets in the lives of young people dramatically encourages and increases the chances of their participation in purposeful, positive, growth-enhancing activities. At the same time, these assets reduce and inhibit their involvement in activities that are most likely to negate or reduce their ability to achieve their potential in life.

These 40 Developmental Assets offer a common-sense, strength-based philosophy that suggests that when you and I witness families and young people in difficulty in our communities, we are not innocent bystanders. We can no longer hide behind the claim we do not have kids of our own, never had kids, or have already had our own kids to worry about. The young people in our communities are a shared responsibility, and we will all be better served when we accept this responsibility.

Search Institute literature suggests success for kids is not simply about education, programs, activities, or organized sports, all of which have an important role to play. Rather, success will be based in our willingness to recognize the need young people have to be guided by boundaries and expectations and to experience safe opportunities that satisfy their natural desire to seek out adventure and risk. Importantly, success for kids is about how we respond to young people's growing desire to be recognized and engaged for what they are: developing adults who have the desire, energy, and talent to change the world for the better.

Young Canadians like Marc and Craig Kielburger and Ryan Hreljic represent the tip of a giant iceberg of underutilized youth-driven talent, innovation, and leadership (for more on them, see chapter 6). Worldwide, these potential leaders are awaiting our invitation to help address the family, community, and global challenges that adults have not, and will never, effectively resolve on their own.

Children and young people today must be given opportunity to find out how they can be accepted, respected, and cherished by their peers and the important adults in their lives. They need and deserve a chance to learn and share the wonderment of community service and, above all, earn and experience the intangible rewards that come from doing something that is truly significant and appreciated by others.

They need to learn how to excel with grace and lose with dignity, to appreciate the humiliation suffered by those among them who appear lonely, overweight, clumsy, or are perceived to be different. Contrary to some people's misconceptions, they want to sit and talk in the presence of men and women intent on helping them to see things they might never see except through another's eyes. Above all, youth need to be surrounded by wise people who share their stories, successes, disappointments, and challenges in a way that is real and reinforces the notion that one of the greatest failures in life is not so much aiming too high and falling short as it is not having the courage, confidence, and support to try in the first place.

Not surprisingly, it will be toward such mentors—positive, innovative, enthusiastic, caring, and engaging—that our children and young people will most frequently be drawn, not because of their position in life, their wealth, or their mandate, but because they find in these people a sense of passion that causes our kids to want to be like them.

To help you grasp this abstract notion of what young people are looking for from us, here is a story of a young boy who ran away from home, leaving a letter behind on the kitchen table explaining to his mom and dad what compelled him to leave. The letter appeared on the editorial page of the *Kansas City Star* many years ago. It was given to the newspaper by the boy's distraught mom, who found it on the morning he ran away. She told the editor "she just hoped it would help other parents who might be wondering about what their kids might be thinking."

Dear Mom & Dad,

Thank you for everything but I am going to Chicago and try to start some kind of a new life. You asked me why I did those things and why I gave you so much trouble and the answer is easy for me to give you, but I'm wondering if you will understand.

Remember when I was about six or seven and I used to want you to just listen to me? I remember all the nice things you gave me for Christmas and my birthday and I was real happy with the things for about a week at the time I got them, but the rest of the time during the year I really didn't want presents ... I just wanted all the time for you to listen to me like I was somebody who felt things too, because I remember even when I was young I felt things. But you said you were too busy.

And Mom, you are a wonderful cook and you had everything so clean and you were tired so much of the time doing all those things that made you busy, but do you know something, Mom? I would have liked crackers and peanut butter just as well ... if you had only had time to sit down with me a little while during the day and said to me: "Tell me all about it so I can maybe help you understand."

And when Donna came I couldn't understand why everyone made so much fuss because I didn't think it was my fault that her hair is curly and her teeth so white and she doesn't have to wear glasses with such thick lenses. Her grades in school were better too, weren't they? I remember that.

If Donna ever has any children, I hope you tell her to just pay some attention to the one that doesn't smile very much because that one will be really crying inside. And when she's about to bake six dozen cookies to make sure first that the kids don't want to tell her about a dream or a hope or something ... because thoughts are important too to small kids even though they don't have so many words when they tell about what they have inside them.

I think that all the kids who are doing so many things that the grown-ups are tearing their hair out worrying about are really looking for somebody that will have the time to listen a few minutes and who would really and truly treat them as they would a grown-up who might be useful to them ... you know ... polite to them.

If you folks had ever said to me, "Pardon me," when you interrupted me, I'd have dropped dead. If somebody asks you where I am, please tell them I've gone looking for somebody with time to listen … because I have a lot of things I want to talk about.

Love to all, your son, Michael

This letter holds an important message for all of us. It is a reminder that we are surrounded every day by children and young people who have a lot of things they want to talk about. We can make a lasting difference in their lives if we will simply take the time to listen, as the next story illustrates.

The Wisdom of a Garbage Man

This story has played a key role for me in convincing thousands of people of the amazing opportunity that exists for all of us to become life-changing influences in the lives of our kids. As a storyteller, this is the one tale I am most frequently asked to tell. It speaks to the opportunity we all have every day to make a difference.

The story came into my life while I was attending an international conference in Denver, Colorado. That was more than three decades ago and as my memory has declined, accuracy of the narrative may be somewhat compromised. Yet to this day, after over thirty years of telling it, I get asked repeatedly to "Tell it again."

As with most conference goers, back in Denver I was attempting to select the best presenters. Many readers will have experienced this same challenge. What is a conference delegate to do when faced with a long list of concurrent sessions? Do you scan the conference program, count the number of degrees speakers have after their name, and then go listen to those with the most? My advice: don't do it! Do you determine how many books presenters have written and then multiply that by the number of degrees they hold? Don't do that either, because, as I have learned, some experts can write well but not speak; others speak well but cannot write.

During this admittedly imperfect evaluation process, I spotted the briefest speaker description in the entire conference program: just three words—James Michener, Author. I had read and loved many of his books, and since I had found no effective way of evaluating the potential of other presenters, I decided to take a chance. That is how I ended up in a packed room of people whose motivation for being there probably mirrored my own. Could James Michener speak as well as he wrote, we all wondered, and why was he speaking to professional youth workers at a conference on how to enhance the lives of young people?

Maybe two minutes after the scheduled start time, the then sixty-seven-year-old James Michener appeared, slowly advancing down the side aisle. His entry was made more resplendent by his magnificent head of white hair, as he walked slowly up and across the stage. No podium, no introduction, no notes; just a wooden stool at the front edge of the stage, where he proceeded to park himself and then do a slow and penetrating 180-degree scan of the audience, which resulted in an ominous silence. You could have heard the proverbial pin drop.

He began: "I think I know why many of you are here. You want to find out why a lowly author has come to a conference of professionals who work with young people and their families every day. For you to better understand why I'm here, it occurs to me there are probably some things about James Michener that you may not know.

"Maybe you don't know that I grew up in the small town of Doylestown, Pennsylvania. I'll bet you didn't know that. I remember the Friday afternoon a couple of days before my seventh birthday when a social worker picked me up and took me to what I think was my fourth foster home in seven years. I'll bet you didn't know that either! I remember, though, because changing foster homes was always hard. The worker spent an hour introducing me to my new foster parents, and then it was time for her to leave and for me to sit down for my first dinner with my newest foster mom and dad, two people I'd known for only sixty minutes. At the end of that meal, I knew two important things about my new foster parents.

"First of all, I thought they kind of liked me and that we were going to get along okay together. My second impression was that they were the poorest foster parents I'd ever had. They told me they both had full-time jobs during the week but they couldn't make enough money to pay the rent and put food on the table, so every Saturday and Sunday they worked around the community cleaning other people's homes and doing their laundry. Because they didn't have any money to pay for entertainment for me and didn't know other young families where I could go to play, I was told I'd have to stay home by myself on weekends while they worked.

"I remember that first Saturday morning in my new foster home. It was the worst Saturday morning of my life. I just wandered from room to room—no one to talk to, no one to listen to me. I finally decided to go sit outside on the back steps. That was a good move, because for about an hour I just sat and watched the wind swirling dust up through the tomato and potato plants. That was the most exciting thing I'd seen all morning.

"Then I heard a truck coming down the alley and that was interesting, because I'd never lived in a foster home with an alley behind it. I decided to wait and see what kind of a truck goes down back alleys on Saturdays.

"I waited and waited because I could hear it getting closer and closer, and it finally stopped right behind our house. I knew right away it was a garbage truck because I'd seen pictures of them and watched them driving around town, but I'd never seen one operate. I watched carefully. The garbage man left the engine running, climbed out of the cab, went back and dumped our garbage in the truck, and then he climbed back into the cab and drove away.

"That night at dinner I told my foster parents what I'd seen and they told me it happened every Saturday. I remember telling them I'd be back out there again next Saturday, because now I knew what he was supposed to do and I wanted to be sure he did it right.

"That second Saturday I was really disappointed because by noon the garbage truck hadn't come. I was afraid to go back in the house for the sandwich my parents had put in the icebox for me because I might miss him. Finally, about two o'clock, I heard a truck in the distance and I knew it was him.

"He finally pulled up behind our house and I watched carefully as he went through the same routine: engine running, back to dump the garbage, climb back in the truck, and drive away.

"Well, to make this story a bit shorter, it was Saturday number three and there had been no change in my financial situation and I still hadn't found any new friends. Once again, I was sitting on the back steps waiting for the garbage man. I was disappointed because by three o'clock he still hadn't come and I thought maybe there had been a change in his schedule.

"Just when I was about to give up, I heard a truck in the distance and knew it was him. I remember it was almost four o'clock when he finally drove up and I watched him go through the same familiar actions, but this time when he finished, he climbed back into the cab, reached over, and turned off the ignition. Then he climbed back down, opened up our back gate, and walked down the path to where I was sitting and asked, 'What's your name?'

"I told him, 'My name is Jimmy Michener, I'm seven years old, and I'm kind of lonely. I don't have anyone to talk to.' He sat down beside me on the stairs and told me he had been thinking about me for the past three weeks, that it didn't make sense for him to drive that dumb garbage truck up and down the alleys and not take a few minutes so we could sit down and talk and maybe learn things from one another."

Michener went on to explain: "For two years the garbage man came almost every Saturday. Sometimes he was busy and he would only stay for ten minutes, but other times when there was something important to talk about, he would stay for an hour. I remember we talked about everything that's important to small kids. Pets, war, peace, school, books, sports, girls, fishing, and politics. He would listen to anything I was interested in and then would share his wisdom and experience.

"On that third Saturday I remember, as he left, he said to me, 'Jimmy Michener, I would know and understand you better if during the week you would write stories about yourself, store them in your mind, and then tell them to me when we get together.' My friends, I began to develop my interest and skill in writing by telling stories to a garbage man over sixty years ago on the back steps of my foster home."

He concluded: "As many of you realize, I've grown up to be a fairly well known writer. I have personally met and known every American president in my lifetime. I have travelled throughout the world in the course of writing my books and met kings, queens, presidents, and world leaders. Not one of those important people contributed as much to who I am, what I believe, what I value, how I treat people, and what I write in my books as did that garbage man who knew, and cared about, how a lonely kid felt in a back alley in Doylestown, Pennsylvania, sixty years ago."

There is a vitally important lesson in James Michener's story for all of us concerned with the well-being of boys and girls today. Within each of us lies the potential to change the world for the better for all young people if we will simply take the time every day to demonstrate "the wisdom of a garbage man."

The responsibility of raising healthy kids rests not solely with parents, who, often with little or no experience, no formal training, and certainly no accompanying standard operating procedures, find themselves faced with the most complex, demanding, and sometimes frustrating challenge of their lives: that of parenting happy, responsible kids. In raising this next future generation what matters is what each of us can do every day, for little more than the thought and time it takes. I used to think that making a difference in a child's life had to involve untold hours of time and commitment. And then the reality hit me. Coach Nick Turik changed my life in ten minutes. Mrs. Simpson redirected me from a truant's fishing expedition and back to school with seven words delivered in a matter of seconds. In the chapters to follow, you'll learn how these kinds of caring people, like yourself, have dramatically changed the lives of young people for the better through time spent that can be measured in seconds, minutes, and, if they chose, sometimes hours, months, years, or a lifetime.

LESSONS TO TAKE AWAY

1. For generations, society has tried to counter the social ills facing children, youth, and families, but problems persist.

2. Search Institute's 40 Developmental Assets offer you a research-based framework of "life building blocks" you can deploy every day to have a positive impact on young people.

3. Youth today, more than ever, are in need of adult mentors with energy, passion, and, most of all, the time to listen.

Chapter 4

Family—We All
Need One

Call it a clan, call it a network, call it a tribe, call it a family.
Whatever you call it, whoever you are, you need one.
—JANE HOWARD, Families

F AMILY STRUCTURES ARE COMPLICATED these days. We are
two-parent, single-parent, blended, stepfamilies, heterosexual,
bisexual, unisexual, grandparents, foster parents, teen parents,
and some of us are parenting our own parents in the midst of
some of the foregoing variations. But both common sense and
family research suggest that family structure is not the most
important thing. What matters is how effectively and successfully your family unit understands and fulfills the responsibility it
has to raise healthy kids who manage to acquire the desire, tools,
confidence, and support they need to achieve their potential in a
world of exponential social change.

It helps to be aware of the social environment in which this
all happens, so let us briefly examine some of the research that
tells us what the Canadian family looks like in the twenty-first
century. A quick glance at recent research by the Vanier Institute
of the Family offers interesting insights. The following statistics

are excerpted from *Fascinating Families,* issue 41, and presented as a bulleted list for readability.

- Statistics Canada predicts that 40.7% of all marriages taking place in 2008 will have ended in divorce by 2035....

- In 2008, the average duration of a marriage that ended in divorce was 14.5 years....

- According to the 2006 General Social Survey, a similar number of people ended common-law unions as did those that ended marriages from 2001 to 2006.

- While the granting of a divorce marks the dissolution of a relationship,... the divorce represents a larger process of changing relationships for all involved, most especially the couple and any children....

- Dealing with family change can be very difficult, and existing supports are often inadequate to support those involved [to] navigate the personal and legal challenges involved.

A report released in 2010 by the Vanier Institute, titled *Families Count: Profiling Canada's Families IV,* offered other noteworthy statistics. Though based on 2006 census data, this research underscores the fact that ongoing changes in our family structures will continue to be a major factor in the lives of Canadians.

- "Married with children" families now make up 39% ... versus 55% of the population in 1981.

- 18.6% of children live with only one of their parents and 14.6% of children live in a common-law family.

- Common-law families in 1981 made up but 5.6% of Canadian families, but now make up 15.5%.

- Increasing numbers of kids are living in blended stepfamilies....

- In 1981, fully 81% of Canadian kids under 15 were living with legally married parents. By 2006, only 66% of kids under 15 were living with legally married parents.

Some researchers have extrapolated that as many as four in ten children who live with their mom and dad today will not be living with the same set of parents ten years from now.

Besides the changing landscape for families, we need to appreciate the seemingly overwhelming influence of technological change on the lives of adults and children. In the past ten years there has been a dramatic increase in children's access to television, the Internet, text messaging, video games, cellphones, and social networking. By themselves, these technologies are neither simply bad nor good. If, like smoking, exposure to technology was categorically bad, it would be simple to tell our kids: just don't do it! But, of course, it's *not* all bad. Television can offer access to excellent educational opportunities, cellphones can enhance parent-child/teen communication and safety, and the Internet opens new ways of learning and affordable tutoring right in kids' own homes or libraries.

For these reasons it's important to weigh the positives with the negatives that can be drawn from studies such as the Vanier Institute's *Good Servant, Bad Master?* (2007), by Arlene Moscovitch, which examines the influence of electronic media on Canadian children and families. Here are a few of those findings:

- Communications technologies have become such an essential element of our everyday lives that some researchers now define homes as "media hubs."

- More family members, beginning at ever younger ages, are using "newer," more interactive technologies, including the Internet and mobile phones.

- People within families are using these technologies in increasingly individualistic contexts.... Already-busy families seem to be interacting in more fragmented ways, with fewer communal activities.

- For many young people, multi-tasking has become the norm, as they toggle between different communications devices and experiences....

- Communication devices can help family members connect on a day-to-day basis. They also serve as unparalleled vehicles for commercial interests to get their messages out to ever-younger "markets" and their often-captive parents.

I recommend perusing this report for further statistics on media use that may surprise you—or may not—but will certainly reinforce your awareness of our media-saturated world.

Taking a Strength-Based Approach

Your challenge as parents raising healthy and responsible young people will be met within this ever-increasing plurality of family structures and the presence of a widening and deepening media "net." And perhaps needless to say, given the diverse types of "family" today, the notion of the traditional nuclear family as the most prominent source of successful child-rearing is outdated. Overwhelming evidence suggests that healthy children will continue to thrive when they bond with honest, respectful, and caring adults, regardless of how those adults choose to form relationships with others in the raising of children.

Of course, for children living in an abusive home or in a family ravaged by violence, drugs, or alcohol, it would be difficult to defend family structure over the destructive behaviour and turmoil they witness every day. And we should admire and support the courage and devotion of single parents who are effectively raising children alone, motivated by their commitment to teach and model self-sufficiency, tolerance, fairness, and responsibility to their children every day. Such situations reveal yet again that it is not so much the makeup of a family that matters to kids. What is paramount to them is what the adults in their lives do with the family structure they have chosen or are experiencing.

Because of that, this book is written for women and men living in both traditional and non-traditional family structures. I have tried to provide information that can be adapted to any environment in which you are raising children. It is a book written for you and your family of record, that important network of role models and champions every boy and girl needs and deserves. This chapter in particular is addressed to parents and others directly involved in raising children, who seek answers to the important question: What are the most essential things we can do to make sure our clan or network is achieving or exceeding its mandate in helping young members to achieve their potential?

I encourage you to deploy a strength-based approach in making that assessment. Focus first of all on your achievements. My experience with families tells me you will be pleasantly surprised at what you learn when you do a quick appraisal of what you are doing right. If you are someone who needs to put your findings to paper, simply grab a pencil and begin to list what you like most about what you are doing as a parent, a grandparent, neighbour, or family friend. If you're a non-parent, simply delete "my" from the following list. Be sure to get the kids in your life involved in this exercise. Make the assessment easy, non-threatening, and non-judgemental.

Look for the subtle stuff you do. For example, your list might include:

- I say please and thank you when I ask my children for cooperation.

- I know and remember the names of my children's friends.

- I am constructively involved in my children's schooling.

- I give each of my kids a hug every day.

- I tell my kids I trust them and give them responsibility accordingly.

- I admit my mistakes.

- I teach my children honesty and tolerance by being honest and tolerant myself.

- I find time to hear their stories, tell them mine, and learn together.

Remember, the key here is to start off by naming the things you are doing well.

Once you have made a quick mental note or written list of what you are doing right, make a similar assessment of the things you son or daughter is doing right. Better still, do it with them. Maybe they sometimes offer to help around the house, perhaps they work hard at school, treat neighbours and family respectfully, laugh a lot, do their homework, get to school on time, or help care for siblings and pets.

Share the lists you come up with your kids. Take the time to tell them you are proud of how they are doing in school or a particular sport or activity, in choosing friends, or in being uniquely themselves. The importance of this exercise is that when we focus on catching our kids doing something well, it prevents us from falling into that tempting trap of focusing on what our kids are doing wrong. As the lyrics of a very old Johnny Mercer song say, "You've got to accentuate the positive / eliminate the negative," by acknowledging and reinforcing the things your kids are doing right. If you are unclear about where to start with your list, you will find a wealth of ideas, checklists, and practical information in the pages to follow.

Why this focus on the positive? Well, I don't know about you, but I would hate to be judged by my wife solely on the basis of my bitchiest day, by my kids on the basis of my most sarcastic comment, or by my God on the basis of my worst sin. Yet we sometimes do this with our children. We focus on the little, annoying things they inevitably do, at the expense of seeing and celebrating the admirable behaviours that warrant acknowledgement and praise.

Sure, it is annoying when your kids forget to take their shoes off at the front door or walk by the garbage at the back door for the umpteenth time or leave clothing or towels all over the bathroom floor. Of course, these deficiencies should be addressed. However, are they really more important than acknowledging the kindness a son or daughter shows toward a friend, their offer to help wash the dishes, or maybe just the simple fact they helped take care of their younger brother or sister? We are not talking about an either/or stance here, just a fair balance. In this context, an old Irish proverb bears repeating: "As you ramble through life, my friend, no matter what your goal; keep your eye upon the doughnut and not upon the hole." As you reflect on the positives in your life and in your child's life, try to keep *your* eye upon the doughnut.

In today's sometimes hectic world of play dates, school, music lessons, sports, chores, and quality-time-together schedules, also remember that our kids need time to simply be themselves: to watch the spray from a garden hose, gaze in wonderment at the moon ... and share a quiet moment with friends in places not surrounded by KEEP OFF or DO NOT DISTURB signs. Like you and I, kids need time to reflect on who they are and who they might become.

Here is one of the simplest and most effective ideas families have shared with me and which I have been told has resulted in dramatically improved parent-child understanding and relationships. The idea came from a father who had chosen to participate for the second time in a workshop I facilitated. He spoke up when we were talking about finding better ways to improve communication between young people and the adults in their family.

He began by explaining he had attended a similar workshop I had led the year before. He left that workshop committed to improving his and his wife's connection with their kids. He explained he had taken home from the workshop a simple checklist that offered opportunity for his teens to share their perception of, among other things, how well their family communicated. Sitting around the dinner table at the end of a meal that night, he asked his wife and teenage son and daughter if they wanted to try a simple test he had learned at the workshop. He explained it was designed to help families determine how well they communicated. He told us in introducing the idea to his family he could not resist adding, "We must be pretty good at it, because look at what we're doing right now."

He then told us that simple comment from him had led to an uncomfortable silence, broken when his seventeen-year-old daughter said, "Dad, we don't communicate in this house. You give orders. Sometimes you try to tell us what we should think and believe without listening to our opinion." His slightly younger son chimed in, "That's true, Dad, you don't listen. You won't even turn off the television when are having dinner together.

"Do you know how bad it is, Dad? Remember about two weeks ago when I was having trouble with math and told you I was worried about an exam? Then do you remember that night at dinner a week later when you asked me how I did on the test? When I told you proudly I got 82 percent, do remember what your response was, Dad? I bet you don't! You pointed to the TV and said, 'Look at that ... it's 3 to 1 for Vancouver.' We don't communicate in this family, Dad."

The father continued his story. "I think my wife and I were visibly shaken. I know I was. Luckily, the kids caught me on a good day because I remember I stood up, walked over, and turned off the TV and went back to the table. I told my wife and kids, no more TV for their dad at dinnertime and that I was sorry for what happened, that it wouldn't happen again."

He explained there followed a long silence until his daughter blurted out, "Well, now that we have all this time on our hands, what are we going to do after we finish eating?" His son offered: "How about if at every meal we eat together, we take time at the end and give each of us three minutes to talk about anything that's important in our lives? Dad, Mom, this means you've got to participate too."

The father went on to explain that by coming to that simple agreement his family had effectively changed their family dynamics for the better—forever. He added, "There really wasn't any need to find any new time in our hectic schedules. It was just a matter of deciding together how we could better use the time we already had to our greatest advantage."

Granted, few families are able to sit around a dinner table every night re-creating experiences like this. The truth is, though, almost all of us could find the ten to twelve minutes it takes to make this kind of opportunity available for parents and kids alike once or twice a week. Here is my by now familiar reminder: Improving family understanding and communication is not so much about finding more time. It's about prioritizing how we spend the time we already have. At its core, this whole notion of raising healthy kids is not based on money or programs or material things. It has more to do with sharing life experiences and relationships, whatever form those take in your life; of finding the time to build them together within your family.

The next chapter, which introduces Search Institute's 40 Developmental Assets, contains many ideas you can choose from and deploy if you and the young people in your life find they resonate for your family. Most of you will discover as well ample evidence that you are already doing many of the "right things." You may also find reason to do them more frequently and more intentionally.

LESSONS TO TAKE AWAY

1. Families today come in many forms. Their structure is not as important as how well they support young members who are striving to achieve their potential.

2. To assess your own family relations, begin by making a list of what parents—and kids—are doing right. Accentuate the positive.

3. To improve parent-child communication, you may need to reprioritize the time already available to you. Improving parent-child communication may mean looking together for new ways to honour important traditions, focusing on strengths, communicating respectfully, and, above all, reminding yourselves that your actions will always speak louder than your words.

Chapter 5

The ABCs of
Asset Building

Much of the work of asset building occurs for free.
It is the stuff people do in their everyday lives.
—PETER L. BENSON, FORMER PRESIDENT/CEO,
SEARCH INSTITUTE

THE 40 DEVELOPMENTAL ASSETS described by Search Institute are as easy to understand as ABC. For most of us they simply restate—in practical, easily understood language—influences we experienced or heard about in our formative years. For many of us the assets offer a chance to revisit important experiences, qualities, and support systems that played a key role in our own development.

These forty assets are frequently referenced in the chapters to follow, and this brief introduction should be all you need to elevate you to the level of Bachelor of Asset Building. Your master's designation will come as you successfully apply this new-found or enhanced knowledge by introducing assets into the lives of children and young people within your sphere of influence.

And so, let's get right to the ABCs of asset building. And of course, when all is said and done, what matters most is that you put into action the how-tos offered in this book, understanding that asset building in the lives of kids cannot happen without you. For that reason, and because of my strong belief in their effectiveness, much of what you will learn in chapters to follow falls into the category of "How you can do it with assets."

What Are Developmental Assets?

Do you ever wonder why some kids seem to grow up with ease while others struggle? Are you surprised that some kids thrive in spite of difficult circumstances? Search Institute is a non-profit research organization in Minneapolis, Minnesota, that has been asking these same questions since 1958. Through studies involving hundreds of thousands of young people across the country, Search Institute has found forty factors that are essential to young people's success. They call these forty factors Developmental Assets. These assets are not financial. Instead, they are opportunities, skills, relationships, values, and self-perceptions that all young people need in their lives. The assets are both external (things that other people provide for youth) and internal (things that young people develop within themselves).

About Search Institute

Search Institute recently reached its fiftieth anniversary year. An article by Patrice Releford in the *Minneapolis Star Tribune* offered one of the most succinct overviews I have seen of the institute's history. With permission I offer her story, published under the following headline: "At Their 50-Year Mark, Search Institute Still Has a Heart for Kids."

Search Institute evolved from a Midwestern youth survey organization in the late 1950s to a nationally renowned child and adolescent development agency in the late 1980s and

1990s. Today, Search Institute resources are used by hundreds of thousands of parents, schools and youth agencies throughout the world.

According to youth development experts, Search Institute's key contribution is a pioneering framework of 40 "developmental assets," or qualities that all kids should possess, whether they live in a penthouse or a tenement. They were developed by Peter L. Benson, Search Institute's president and CEO. At first glance, the non-profit's developmental assets are deceptively simple.

"It's not the only thing we do but our signature contribution is to bring to the world this universal framework [of developmental assets]," Benson said. "Scientific studies show the 40 assets matter for all kids across race, ethnicity and family income and regardless of where they live."

They include the need for a caring school climate, a sense of purpose and strong relationships with at least three non-parent adults. But youth experts said Search Institute's philosophy represented a ground breaking research-backed road map that reshaped the way many schools, governments and other agencies work with youth.

"Before he [Benson] came onto the scene, America defined positive development in young people as the absence of problems," said Richard Lerner, director of the Institute for Applied Research in Youth Development at Tufts University in Boston. "Imagine if your boss said you've done a good job today simply because you didn't embarrass them or burn down the office."...

Search Institute is a pillar of the youth development movement, Lerner said. "In his notion of youth development Benson and Search Institute have given communities and families hands-on actions they can take to improve the lives of young people," Lerner said. "If there was a medal that we gave out in the youth development field, he would be first in line to get one."

Introducing Developmental Assets

The 40 Developmental Assets are evidence-based and above all easily understood. The first time you read the list of assets, they will resonate for you. Most of you will recognize every one of the forty, and many will be able to see where they fit and where they came from in your own lives.

The assets are not intended to replace your current beliefs. They simply serve to reinforce, focus, and explain the sometimes hazy understandings we have of where our own beliefs, values, and biases came from. More importantly, they may give us the confidence and nudge we need to apply our values intentionally to better the lives of every child and young person within our influence.

To reiterate, the assets fall into two main groups: external (things others provide for youth) and internal (things young people develop within themselves). Within each of these groups there are four categories. Here are the categories at a glance, followed by a more detailed breakdown of the total list:

EXTERNAL ASSETS	INTERNAL ASSETS
SUPPORT	COMMITMENT TO LEARNING
EMPOWERMENT	POSITIVE VALUES
BOUNDARIES AND EXPECTATIONS	SOCIAL COMPETENCIES
CONSTRUCTIVE USE OF TIME	POSITIVE IDENTITY

EXTERNAL ASSETS

SUPPORT

Young people need to be supported, cared for, and loved by their families and many others. They also need organizations and institutions, such as schools and faith-based organizations, that provide positive, supportive environments. There are six Support assets:

1   **Family support** | Family life provides high levels of love and support.

2   **Positive family communication** | Young person and her or his parent(s) communicate positively, and young person is willing to seek advice and counsel from parent(s).

3   **Other adult relationships** | Young person receives support from three or more non-parent adults.

4   **Caring neighbourhood** | Young person experiences caring neighbours.

5   **Caring school climate** | School provides a caring, encouraging environment.

6   **Parent involvement in schooling** | Parent(s) are actively involved in helping young person succeed in school.

EMPOWERMENT

Young people need to feel that their community values them and that they have important ways to contribute. They must also feel safe. There are four Empowerment assets:

7   **Community values youth** | Young person perceives that adults in the community value youth.

8   **Youth as resources** | Young people are given useful roles in the community.

9   **Service to others** | Young person serves in the community one hour or more per week.

10 **Safety** | Young person feels safe at home, at school, and in the neighbourhood.

BOUNDARIES AND EXPECTATIONS

Young people need to know what is expected of them and whether activities and behaviours are acceptable or not acceptable. There are six Boundaries and Expectations assets:

11 **Family boundaries** | Family has clear rules and consequences and monitors the young person's whereabouts.

12 **School boundaries** | School provides clear rules and consequences.

13 **Neighbourhood boundaries** | Neighbours take responsibility for monitoring young people's behaviour.

14 **Adult role models** | Parent(s) and other adults model positive, responsible behaviour.

15 **Positive peer influence** | Young person's best friends model responsible behaviour.

16 **High expectations** | Both parent(s) and teachers encourage the young person to do well.

CONSTRUCTIVE USE OF TIME

Young people need to spend their time in positive, healthy ways. This includes doing activities in youth programs, in faith-based institutions, and at home. There are four Constructive Use of Time assets:

17 **Creative activities** | Young person spends three or more hours per week in lessons or practice in music, theatre, or other arts.

18 **Youth programs** | Young person spends three or more hours per week in sports, clubs, or organizations at school and/or in the community.

19 **Religious community** | Young person spends one or more hours per week in activities in a religious institution.

20 **Time at home** | Young person is out with friends "with nothing special to do" two or fewer nights per week.

INTERNAL ASSETS

COMMITMENT TO LEARNING

Young people do best when they develop a strong interest in and commitment to education and learning. There are five Commitment to Learning assets:

21 **Achievement motivation** | Young person is motivated to do well in school.

22 **School engagement** | Young person is actively engaged in learning.

23 **Homework** | Young person reports doing at least one hour of homework every school day.

24 **Bonding to school** | Young person cares about her or his school.

25 **Reading for pleasure** | Young person reads for pleasure three or more hours per week.

POSITIVE VALUES

Young people thrive when they develop strong values that guide their choices. There are six Positive Values assets:

26 **Caring** | Young person places high value on helping other people.

27 **Equality and social justice** | Young person places high value on promoting equality and reducing hunger and poverty.

28 **Integrity** | Young person acts on convictions and stands up for her or his beliefs.

29 **Honesty** | Young person "tells the truth even when it is not easy."

30 **Responsibility** | Young person accepts and takes personal responsibility.

31 **Restraint** | Young person believes it is important not to be sexually active or to use alcohol or other drugs.

SOCIAL COMPETENCIES

Young people benefit from having skills and competencies that equip them to make positive choices, to build relationships, and to deal with difficult situations. Five assets make up the category of Social Competencies:

32 **Planning and decision making** | Young person knows how to plan ahead and make choices.

33 **Interpersonal competence** | Young person has empathy, sensitivity, and friendship skills.

34 **Cultural competence** | Young person has knowledge of and comfort with people of different cultural/racial/ethnic backgrounds.

35 **Resistance skills** | Young person can resist negative peer pressure and dangerous situations.

36 Peaceful conflict resolution | Young person seeks to resolve conflict non-violently.

Positive Identity

Young people need to develop a strong sense of their own power, purpose, worth, and promise. There are four Positive Identity assets:

37 Personal power | Young person feels he or she has control over "things that happen to me."

38 Self-esteem | Young person reports having a high self-esteem.

39 Sense of purpose | Young person reports that "my life has a purpose."

40 Positive view of personal future | Young person is optimistic about her or his personal future.

The Power of Developmental Assets

Here is where you will see compelling graphic evidence that the more assets children and young people have in their lives, the greater the likelihood of their involvement in life-enhancing behaviours, accompanied by a significantly reduced risk of them engaging in activities that can deplete their potential. For more about Developmental Assets, see the book's appendix.

PROMOTING POSITIVE ATTITUDES AND BEHAVIOURS*

Having more Developmental Assets increases the chances that young people will have positive attitudes and behaviours. Search Institute research has found that young people with more assets are more likely to participate in eight positive behaviours. Here are some examples:

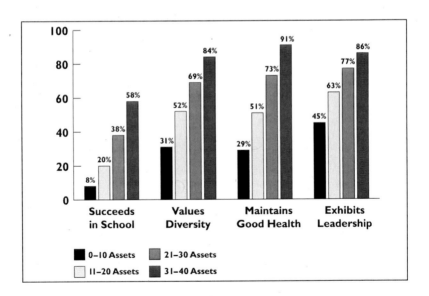

THE POWER OF ASSETS TO PROTECT*

Assets can help protect young people from making many harmful and unhealthy choices. Youth with more assets are less likely than youth with fewer assets to engage in twenty-four risky behaviours, such as tobacco use, gambling, violence, and shoplifting. This chart shows this relationship:

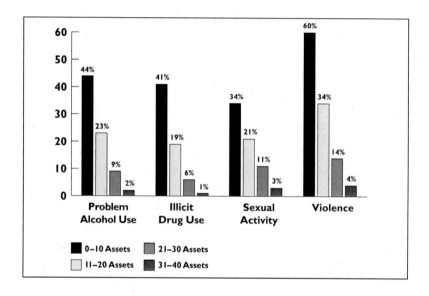

* Based on data from the *Search Institute Profiles of Student Life: Attitudes and Behaviors* survey; gathered in 2010 from almost 90,000 students in Grades 6 to 12 (ages approximately 11 to 18) from 111 communities in 26 U.S. states.

Frequently Asked Questions

Search Institute has found that some questions about the asset framework come up again and again. Here are answers to a number of them:

1. I don't have kids, and I don't work with kids—can I build assets?

   Yes! One of the most important messages of asset building is that everyone plays a role, not just families, youth workers, and teachers. The assets offer ways everyone can provide the positive relationships and experiences young people need. For some, it may be as simple as smiling and saying hello to young people encountered during daily activities. For others, it could mean developing a significant relationship with a young person. Even using the asset framework to assess candidates for public office can be a way of supporting asset building.

2. Are resources on the assets available in any other language?

   Yes. Search Institute has several resources in Spanish, including the list of forty assets. This list is also available in French. When distributing the list, consider using English on one side and Spanish or French on the other, depending on the languages spoken in your area.

3. Do younger children need the same assets as teenagers?

   The Developmental Assets framework applies to all ages. The core of each asset is important to children of all ages but experienced, built, and defined differently at different stages of development. Search Institute has developed frameworks for early childhood (ages 3 to 5), middle childhood (ages 8 to 12), and adolescents (ages 12 to 18), and researchers continue to work on defining the assets for children of all ages.

4. How important is it that I focus on each individual asset?

While each individual asset is critical to development, it's more important (and easier!) to pay attention to the eight categories of assets and the broader concepts of external assets and internal assets.

5. What's the best way to develop an understanding of the assets?

Share your ideas, questions, suggestions, stories, and frustrations with others. Talk about how the forty assets work in your own experience, and how they connect to your own values and ideals.

6. Once a young person has a particular asset, does he or she have it forever?

No. Assets can come and go, based on current relationships and experiences. They need to be built throughout a person's life.

7. Is it important for asset-building initiatives to find ways to exemplify the asset focus in our structure, meetings, and planning?

Yes! This is a great way to reinforce people's understanding of the assets, and it can also lead to stronger teams and organizations. For example, some organizations use the eight categories of assets to look at how they work together, asking questions like: How can we support each other? What should be our boundaries and expectations for meetings? and so on.

8. Are some assets more important than others?

    Don't pick and choose assets—the power of this framework lies in how they work together. Young people need as many of the assets as they can get. If you want to focus specific attention on one or two assets at a time, do so with the reminder that they are only part of the larger framework.

9. Is it OK to focus on just the assets that seem most critical for our kids?

    Yes. You can use the asset framework to help set priorities in your community. For example, some communities have looked at the framework and realized they haven't done much to address issues of boundaries. Others have found that there are few opportunities for young people to be involved in constructive activities.

10. A lot of activities are "asset building," but few people have heard of the concept. How can we get other "asset builders" on board?

    Celebrate, affirm, and honour the ways people already build assets (even if they don't call it that). A good way to first get people excited is to have them go through the list and mark what they're already doing. People and organizations that build assets can also be acknowledged and featured in your community newspaper or other public forum.

11. Does having more assets just reduce risk-taking behaviours?

    No. The assets also promote positive outcomes and positive behaviour, such as academic success, leadership skills, and healthy lifestyle.

12. Do we have to create a new program based on asset building?

No. You can use the asset framework to help evaluate and improve existing programs and opportunities for young people. For example: How can a focus on assets improve meetings? How can it enhance what's happening in a 4-H group? How can it impact a community-wide celebration?

13. Can a single action help to build more than one of the assets?

Certainly! For example, a caring relationship with an adult (asset 3) can lead to many of the other assets, including Community Values Youth (asset 7), Adult Role Models (asset 14), and Self-Esteem (asset 38).

THE GAP IN ASSETS AMONG YOUNG PEOPLE

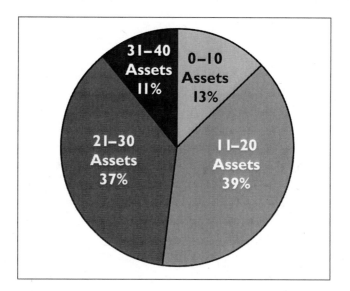

Experience tells me that armed with this information about Developmental Assets, you can with confidence become more intentional and increasingly effective and significant in the lives of all children within your influence. The next chapter reveals that while adults building assets in the lives of young people remains of highest priority, children and young people throughout the world also have a role to play. They too are building assets in the lives of their siblings, friends, classmates, and teammates. Stories of their achievements are often moving, sometimes humorous, and always compelling.

LESSONS TO TAKE AWAY

1. The signature contribution of Search Institute is a framework of 40 Developmental Assets—qualities that can contribute to the healthy development of all kids.

2. The 40 Developmental Assets list opportunities, skills, relationships, values, and self-perceptions that matter to all young people, regardless of race, ethnicity, family income, or geographic location.

3. Research indicates that the presence of assets can help protect young people from making harmful and unhealthy choices at the same time that they promote positive outcomes and behaviour.

Chapter 6

Kids Can Be
Asset Builders Too

> *We must remember that one determined person can*
> *make a significant difference, and that a small group of*
> *determined people can change the course of history.*
> —SONIA JOHNSON

W AIT A MINUTE! WAIT JUST A MINUTE!" I hear you saying. First you tell us one of the most important things we can do for the children in our lives is to intentionally enhance and increase the 40 Developmental Assets available to them. Now you are trying to tell us that those same kids have the capacity to build assets in the lives of people in their lives?

Short answer: Yes, those seemingly contradictory points are both true. Let me explain. A few years ago, shortly after I was introduced to Search Institute's Asset Approach, I received a call from the Kamloops Society for Alcohol and Drug Services, a community-based program focusing on prevention and awareness in my hometown of Kamloops, British Columbia, today a city of 87,000 in the province's interior. Their request was simple but intriguing. They were looking for a new way of introducing Drug Awareness Week to elementary students within the Kamloops

School District. Event planners were being understandably cautious in testing the notion of taking a more positive approach, and they had decided to start with a single class of Grade 5 and 6 students.

The idea appealed to me for several reasons. First of all, I liked their notion of focusing on positives rather than negatives, of moving away from the simple "Just Say No" edict, which in the experience of many had failed miserably to change kids' attitudes toward substance use and abuse. Naturally, the possibility of returning to my hometown to spend time with youngsters in the same school system from which I had derived such benefit and fun had a resounding appeal as well. It was agreed that I would spend an hour and a half with approximately thirty 11- and 12-year-olds talking about a topic the organizers and I thought might work: "How kids can change the world for the better, every day, for nothing but the time it takes."

I arrived in Kamloops on the night prior to meeting those young students. The planning committee had suggested we get together for an hour that evening to make certain everything was in order. That is when they told me there had been a bit of a change in plans. Word had spread throughout the elementary school system that some guy from the city was coming to Kamloops to tell kids how they could change the world. It seems the news that someone thought kids could change the world had had a snowball effect. Instead of thirty Grade 5 and 6 students, there would now be over 330, and the venue had changed from a school classroom to the Sagebrush Theatre at the local high school.

That is how I found myself on a stage peering out at three hundred–plus restless souls who had gathered, one must presume, as a result of either a passing interest or their teacher's directive. I spent the first few minutes talking with the students about the whole idea of Developmental Assets, how every boy and girl could benefit from increasing the number of these life building blocks in their lives. The kids and I talked about how the presence of assets could protect them from the kind of behaviours they do not want and promote the kind they do, the kind that could markedly increase their chances of achieving their potential in life.

When the fidgeting reached earthquake proportions, I resorted to an interactive technique I had initially prepared for a classroom of thirty. It entailed handing out single sheets of paper that kind of exploded into the hands of every young person in that auditorium. Here is what the handout said:

"I believe I can make a difference!"

When I leave this workshop today and return to my classroom, my family and my community, I plan to do what?

Please list your ideas in the space below:

_____

_____

_____

_____

_____

_____

_____

So I can help increase the number of assets in the lives of my friends, my brothers and sisters and kids who live in my neighbourhood.

Each sheet contained six lines on which the students could write down their ideas. When they indicated at the end of the allocated five minutes that they needed more time to write, I allowed another five, thinking they were having trouble grasping the concept. When they later begged for "just two minutes, Keith," I concluded this approach was off the mark. Perhaps this concept was too advanced for students of this age. Well, how wrong I was!

When I made my first attempt to gain a sense of how the hundreds of kids in the audience would respond, it became clear that nearly every student had been successful in putting to paper ideas about how they planned to make a difference. Through a quickly contrived and less-than-perfect process, seventeen members of the audience were selected to read their commitments onstage. Time and space limitations compelled us to limit the kids' responses to include only those who had compiled twenty or more ideas in the allocated time.

Those of us who worry about a lack of values, innovation, or sense of responsibility among our future leaders should be heartened by what those youngsters had to offer. In total, completed handouts later tallied showed those 330 youngsters documented over 2,500 ways in which they intended to make a difference. There were, of course, many duplications of ideas, but take cheer in hearing what children declared they would do to make the world a better place.

- I'll go to school and help kids who don't understand questions.

- I'll offer to help little kids tie their shoelaces.

- I'll start giving kids a put-up instead of a put-down.

- I'll stick up for someone younger than me.

- Even if they're an adult, I'll try to help them learn something.

- I'll let them borrow things if they need them.

- I'll never say rude comments.

- I'll give my mom a kiss each day.

- I'll help those who are crying in school.

- I will share my joy. I'll put my arm around a kid who is sad or lonely.

And here is the one I will never forget:

- I'm going to return the toy truck to the little kid I stole it from across the street.

I learned an important lesson that day from those young children who were growing up in my old hometown. They reminded me that kids are not that different from you and me. They want to be seen, they want to be heard, and they need and want a chance to demonstrate their desire and ability to make a difference.

And so, as you reflect on the 40 Developmental Assets, take time to pick out the ones that empower children to join with you in changing the world. They are not hard to find. Here are a few examples:

Asset 4: Caring neighbourhood. Not only can children derive benefit from living in one, they can achieve as much or more from helping build one.

Asset 8: Youth as resources. Keep reminding yourself that kids are part of the solution, not the problem.

Asset 14: Adult role models. It is easy to understand that young people need positive mentors in their lives. It is essential to understand and act on the reality that they, too, can be role models to their friends, siblings, and younger children.

Asset 32: Planning and decision making. Like many of the assets, kids will learn more about this one more from what they experience than what they are told.

The key lesson for all of us as we embark on our asset-building adventure is to recognize that introducing and enhancing the 40 Developmental Assets in the life of every child and young person within your influence can be accomplished in two important ways. First, you can help them identify and enhance assets important to them. Second, you can make them aware of the capacity they have to build assets in the lives of children within *their* influence every day.

The two hours I spent with those Kamloops kids changed forever my perception of and approach toward youth involvement. I remember I used to say glibly to kids, "It would be nice if you would get involved." In the past, I would tell them their participation was important. I don't say that anymore. Today I tell them we as adults will never achieve a more just, compassionate, and tolerant world without their help. I tell organizations and anyone who will listen that if they really want young people to engage in making a difference, they need to involve them from the very beginning. I caution them not to start any important initiative without the active involvement of young people. And I tell them that if they do not involve youth, there is great danger that their initiative will become yet another adult-inspired activity or program with less-than-desired results and an inordinately short lifespan.

Kids Changing the World. We Can't Do It Without Them

Still a bit hesitant? Not quite convinced that young people have a role to play? Here are some young role models to convince and inspire you. Craig Kielburger of Thornhill, Ontario, was twelve years old when he gathered a bunch of his friends and class-mates together in 1996 to form an organization he called Free the Children. It is now an international network aimed at eradicating child slave labour throughout the world.

What got him started? One morning, Craig read a news-paper article about the murder of a twelve-year-old Pakistani boy who had been a slave in a carpet factory since the age of four. Today, Free the Children continues to be led by Craig along with his brother Marc. It is one of the largest children's human rights activist organizations in the world, having opened more than one hundred schools and rehabilitation centres for enslaved and exploited children.

And how about Ryan Hreljac, a six-year-old student in his first year of school in Kentville, Ontario, who learned from his teacher that people were dying because they did not have clean water to drink in Angola, Africa. He thought it would be a good thing if he helped bring them water. It took him four months to raise his first $70. His determination has grown from that $70 raised by doing simple household chores to build a foundation, formed in 2001, that today has completed a total of 630 water and sanitation projects in 16 countries, bringing clean water to over 700,000 people. The Ryan's Well Foundation, driven largely by the efforts of children, has raised millions of dollars. Ryan was recognized by UNICEF as a global youth leader. A recipient of many national and international awards, he says simply, "The most impressive people I've ever met are the other kids who want to help, too."

We must work harder at finding and involving these remark-able young people who want to make a difference. So, next time your five-year-old tells you they want to save the whales, find a cure for cancer, or help people living in poverty, do not do what I would have done years ago—give my kids a gentle pat on the head and tell them we would talk about it when they got older. Today my response to my grandchildren is "What an amazing idea. How can I help you do it?"

Getting the kids within your influence involved in changing the world does not have to be complicated. It does not have to be limited to the big stuff, although it is big when brothers and sisters help one another, participate in household chores, or help a friend, grandparent, or elderly neighbour. It was big for me a few years ago when a group of kids from Newfoundland asked me to help them launch a cookbook they were writing to encourage healthy eating in families. In learning how this one unfolded, you will be reminded how innovative our younger generation can be.

The kids in Newfoundland had decided to write and publish a book called *Cool Kids Healthy Recipe Cookbook*. In what I can only assume was an act of desperation to land on a safe way to find someone to introduce their book, they decided to go right across Canada to me, a guy who lives near the Pacific Ocean, burns toast, and believed until his thirteenth birthday that tapioca came from fish eyes. Talk about weird! Even today, with a head full of grey hair and that minor nutritional misunderstanding corrected, I still do not touch tapioca. I mean, what will people think of eating next, maybe cod cheeks or tongues or something gross like that?

That is how I ended up introducing a book designed to help kids from Newfoundland share with the world what they think about cooking and eating for health, why no boy or girl should miss the fun of planning a menu, measuring, testing, spilling, mixing, blending, or licking the beaters and bowl. The youngest registered contributor to the book was one year old (either she had an authorized agent or is in the process of becoming the world's next Einstein). The oldest contributor remains ageless because kids, in this instance perhaps a teen, like the adults who raise them, do not always want to let it all hang out. They solicited contributions by word of mouth, by phone, e-mail, in their schools, and through a St. John's Boys and Girls Club newsletter. In deference to their recognition of the international enthusiasm all kids seem to have for eating, they invited recipes from any young person who thought they had an irresistible favourite.

All told, more than one hundred young people from throughout Canada and even south of the border talked about food, glorious food—nutritious meals and snacks that rated high on their "yum yum" meter. Oh sure, there were a few recipes that did not quite make the cut and were not included. Fresh fruit covered in whipped cream and chocolate sauce, French fries smothered in gravy, and giant-sized slurpies. Nor did the spelling always pass the *Webster's Dictionary* test but, hey, bad grammar and spelling are not fattening. After all, who wouldn't enjoy a meal of *pusgetti* or a healthy bowl of *ministoney soop?*

This cookbook project was born when a member of the Boys and Girls Club staff in St. John's, Newfoundland, heard, listened to, and acted upon some ideas being kicked around by an informal group of about half a dozen eight- to ten-year-old kids.

You might understandably ask, what is the purpose of these stories and the somewhat protracted evidence offered of the power of kids to make a difference? My friends, it is simply to drive home the point that within every boy and girl within your span of influence lies the potential to participate actively every day in contributing to making the world a better place for all of us. To do that, young people need someone to acknowledge, explain, and magnify their inherent potential.

That someone is you. Take the time to sit down with young people, one at a time, to explore with them how much we need their help in changing the world for the better. Give them examples of important contributions young people have made throughout history, ask for their opinions and ideas, and elicit from them what it is they wish, want, or could do to demonstrate they can make a difference in the lives of others. Remind yourself of the words of the legendary rocker Jerry Garcia: "Somebody's gotta do something and the incredibly pathetic thing is it's gotta be us."

LESSONS TO TAKE AWAY

1. Adults are not the only ones who can build assets for kids and communities. Young people themselves have great potential to make a difference.

2. For kids to be asset builders, it is essential that they be involved from the start in any program or initiative.

3. As Craig and Marc Kielburger (Free the Children), Ryan Hreljac (Ryan's Well Foundation), and so many other young leaders demonstrate, kids have great ideas on ways to make the world a better place. It is up to us to acknowledge, explain, and magnify that potential.

Chapter 7

Hi Keith!
My Name Is Rachael

> *The young, free to act on their initiative,*
> *can lead their elders in the direction of the unknown.*
> —MARGARET MEAD

H I KEITH! MY NAME IS RACHAEL! I'm fourteen years old and I think I can help you make a difference in the world." That is how I first met Rachael (pronounced RA-chel) Dillman, a teen leader whose values, enthusiasm, and commitment have inspired me and countless others. In the spring of 2000, Rachael was one of approximately 120 young leadership students drawn from junior high schools throughout British Columbia attending a two-day leadership retreat designed to encourage and reinforce their demonstrated commitment toward making a difference in their schools and their communities. They were a receptive audience for a grey-haired public speaker and advocate of the notion that kids are an essential part of the solution, not the problem.

My introduction to Rachael came at the conclusion of a one-hour keynote I delivered to what I recall was one of the more rambunctious, keen, and attentive audiences I had stood before in a long time. At the end of many such engagements, some members of the audience step forward to offer their response to my presentation. On this particular day, Rachael was the last in a line of a few young people who came forward to share their reaction and tell me how they might use the information to further their leadership goals. From these ordinary circumstances, Rachael was to become an extraordinary influence in my life.

She walked briskly toward me, her hand extended. She offered a smile that for reasons I still cannot explain, left me with the impression I was standing in the presence of a teen such as I had never met before. Her words, as I recall them, went something like this: "Hi Keith! My name is Rachael Dillman. Do you know how I can become more involved in public speaking? I was very inspired by your talk on the power of building assets in the lives of young people. I think by public speaking I can really help you make a positive difference and change the world. What should I do?"

Somewhat taken aback, I have to admit that I stumbled, verbally anyway. My response was something like this. "Hey, Rachael, it's good to meet you, and I sure need a lot of help." To which she responded, "Keith, I'm being serious, and I want to know what you're going to do about it." It was then I sensed I was indeed in the presence of an unusually determined and articulate young lady. I tried to recover my composure by assuring Rachael I was being serious too but felt at a loss to respond effectively to what for me was her one-of-a-kind request for help. We went on to talk briefly about the reality that I did not even know where she lived and that anything I could do to assist her would only happen with the approval of her parents. Our discussion ended with my suggestion that she think about it for a month and if at the end of that month she remained determined to become a speaker and to help me make a difference, I would find a way to keep my promise to her to do so.

Over the next month, I did not think very often about Rachael, and yet somehow I was not that surprised when my phone rang at home thirty days later. It was Rachael's mother. "Keith, my name is Sylvia Dillman, I'm Rachael's mother. Do you remember Rachael? She's been talking about you for the last month and telling us you've agreed to help her become a public speaker and to let her co-present with you."

"Indeed, Mrs. Dillman, I do remember Rachael." And so it was that I accepted an invitation to have dinner with the Dillman family. In Sylvia's words, "it would give us a chance to know one another better and to decide if this was something we wanted to do." Soon after, I found myself sitting at the dinner table with Rachael's mom and dad and her younger brothers and sisters on the twentieth floor of an apartment building in downtown Vancouver. It was a dinner experience I will never forget. We talked and shared a bit about our history and our values. Above all, Rachael's mother and father asked the questions every responsible parent should pursue with diligence when choosing other adults to become an influence in the lives of their children. I also had my first glimpse of the Dillman family magic so clearly evidenced in the behaviour of their fourteen-year-old daughter.

Near the end of our meal together, Rachael volunteered that she had been asked by her parents to explain an important ritual they practised whenever they gathered together for a family meal. She said every family member sitting around the table was given three minutes of uninterrupted time they had together labelled "What's your story?" time. This was an opportunity for everyone, including Mom and Dad, to talk about anything that had happened during their day or something of importance to them. Simple rules: no judgements, no interruptions, no criticism. As I listened to members of the Dillman family, ranging in age from five to forty-plus, I realized I was getting my first glimpse of where Rachael's values and confidence had come from.

And the evening's revelations did not end there. At the end of the meal, Rachael's mom and dad excused her and me from cleanup and dishes with the explanation, "This is your evening, and you and Keith are free to go sit in the living room and talk about what it is you plan to do together." I remember opening the discussion with something along the lines of "Rachael, tell me what it is you want to do and how you think I can help you accomplish it."

Her response serves as a constant reminder to me of the amazing latent talent of young people to find thoughtful and innovative ways to make the world a better place. She observed that she liked the way I presented and she had figured out the trick I used in framing my words. "Keith, you use stories as a prop to make and emphasize the points you want to make."

"Guilty as charged, Rachael. Guilty as charged," I replied. I told her that most speakers have a ruse they deploy to help them get and hold an audience's attention and asked her if she had ideas about one she might use.

She told me she had thought about that a lot and she had a good one. When she was seven years old, she told me, her parents had taken her to see the musical *Show Boat.* In her words: "I loved it and spent hours learning and singing my favourite songs. One day when Mom and I were coming out of a shopping mall, I spotted a deserted stage set up outside the mall. I'd already learned a song from *Show Boat,* and I asked Mom if I could go up and sing on that stage. When I'd finished a few people had gathered around and a lady came up and told me my singing was beautiful and she gave me two dollars. She told me to keep it as a reminder I should keep on singing. That small act of recognition from a total stranger encouraged me to pursue singing seriously. When I heard a CD of someone singing 'Ave Maria' by Schubert, I learned and practised it by ear and that led to choir practices, musical competitions, and requests for me to sing at weddings and funerals—all because one adult I didn't even know told me I should try and they believed in me.

"I've thought a lot about it, Keith. I'll use my singing to get the attention of audiences. Then I'll tell them it might never have happened were it not for one lady who I'll probably never know who took the time to give me two dollars as a reminder that I should try to keep on singing and that she believed in me."

At this point Rachael asked me if I'd like to hear her sing. I asked whether she wanted me to move over by the piano in the corner of the living room. "No, Keith. I don't need music. I sing *a cappella*. Is there any particular kind of music you like or any language you'd like to hear me sing in? I sing songs in English, Spanish, French, Finnish, Latin, and Gaelic."

By this time I was beginning to wonder what I had gotten myself into, and so came yet another of my somewhat inane and less than adequate responses. "Rachael, you may want to stick with English if I'm to understand what the lyrics are about!" She stood in the centre of the living room and told me one of her favourite and most meaningful songs, "The Impossible Dream," was featured in *Man of La Mancha*. She thought it might be appropriate to introduce or conclude future presentations where we talked about how children and adults together could dream and change the world. Three minutes later I found myself sitting in awe of this fourteen-year-old girl … in fact, spellbound and speechless. Rachael Dillman had one of the most compelling voices with accompanying gestures I had ever witnessed in a vocalist.

From that very humble beginning in the Dillman family living room, over the course of nearly ten years, Rachael was to spend hundreds of hours with me presenting at conferences, at workshops, in schools, and in communities large and small throughout Western Canada. Audiences ranged in number from thousands at a national conference of Search Institute in Minneapolis, Minnesota, to small groups of First Nations children sitting in a circle with her on the floor, listening to her sing and watching in amazement her talent for creating balloon animals, another skill she used to get and retain their attention as they discussed the potential for each of them to make a difference in their families, communities, and in the world.

When Rachael was fifteen years old, she co-chaired a national conference of teens and supporting adults who gathered for three days in Richmond, B.C. The gathering brought together over one hundred teens and their mentors from across Canada. The teens' purpose was to get significant adults in their lives to help them develop a leadership framework for youth. They sought to create important leadership roles for youth to assure that Canadians of all ages could live in shared respect, tolerance, responsibility, and peace.

Here is an excerpt from an article Rachael wrote in an *Asset Building Networker* newsletter published following that conference.

My family has always given me great support. I can always confide in them when a problem arises, even more so than my friends. And the reasons I've grown up confident, independent, and enthusiastic is the way they raised me. They asked my opinion, gave me responsibility, and trusted me with important decisions. They encouraged me to think and act independently.... I believe I can change the world and that it takes determination, persistence, and hard work to make that a reality. I don't want to be stereotyped as part of the problem just because I'm a teenager.

Adults should look at young people as "clean slates," with hidden potential just waiting to be released.... Important people in my life have always modelled honesty, respect, responsibility, and enthusiasm. They've always had high expectations of me. Mutual trust and honesty are extremely important! When you trust someone and they trust you, you can be given more responsibility and freedom.... I love having the opportunity to talk to audiences—children and adults; to talk to them about how we young people can change the world for the better.

You will not be surprised to learn that this remarkable story does not end there. Rachael graduated from the University of British Columbia in June 2011 with a combined major in political science and economics. She has served as a member's assistant to a cabinet minister in Ottawa. But Rachael cannot let go of her commitment to reaching out to others. I received an e-mail from her a few months ago. She wanted me to know she had set up a mutual support group for young professionals working within the federal government sector in Ottawa. And I thought to myself, "More of the same Rachael." Thankfully her community service is ongoing; her desire to make a difference remains strong.

She ended that e-mail with a request. "As you know, Keith, my sister Anna is now 15 and my brother Lewis is 13. It's important for them to have a chance to make a difference in their community. I'd like you to contact them because I think they'd like to be presenters at some of the workshops you do." And so it was that Rachael's mother, Sylvia, and father Lou and I recently reconnected.

And wouldn't you know it, a couple of months later Supt. Tonia Enger, commanding officer of the North Vancouver RCMP, found herself introducing Rachael's brother and sister as part of a new team of trainers who came together for the first time to speak about the notion of positive tickets (see chapter 9) to an audience of more than one hundred police officers and young people who had volunteered from throughout the North Vancouver public school system. And yes, Rachael, at the end of the couple of hours we had together, Superintendent Enger, I, and all those in the audience agreed it was a pretty good idea you had when you suggested Anna and Lewis be invited to become co-trainers with me. You would have been proud of them.

As you move on to the next chapter about the important role youth organizations can play in the development of healthy children and youth, your commitment to giving young people the opportunity to become leaders in making a difference will give you a solid foundation upon which to frame your expectation of agencies who will matter most to the young people in your life.

LESSONS TO TAKE AWAY

1. Only when we view and involve our children as the essential part of the solution they are will we achieve the just and compassionate society we seek.

2. Teaching children and young people in isolation how they should relate and communicate with their elders is destined to fail. Kids, like their elders, will learn these things best by talking with—not about—each other.

3. By including one or more young people in your efforts to improve intergenerational understanding and respect, you too might experience the youth leadership Margaret Mead referred to in the quote that opened this chapter.

Chapter 8

What to Look For in Youth Organizations

Those who know only what they do, tend to work harder.
Those who know why they do, tend to work smarter.
—SIMON SINEK, Start with Why: How Great
Leaders Inspire Everyone to Take Action

S O FAR I HAVE SHARED EXAMPLES of the difference *individuals* can make in our kids' lives. Organizations serving youth hold that same potential when they become partners with parents by offering relationships, activities, and role modelling. In doing so they give every boy and girl a chance to learn and practise new life and interpersonal skills, experience new challenges, participate in group and team activities, and, above all, acquire and demonstrate their own capacity to lead. Note that although this chapter deals mostly with organizations, hence is addressed chiefly to readers affiliated with such groups, it identifies a central role for parents, who may wish to stay tuned.

The children and teens who walk through the doors of youth agencies today bring with them the same vital blend of energy, hope, complexity, delight, and potential that has characterized generations of kids throughout history. Today's young people also come from a world with unprecedented access to knowledge, the good and evil of exploding information networks, and altered family structures. As always, they have a commendable need and desire to demonstrate their goodness and talent to a world that should be seeking their participation at every opportunity.

These technology-savvy kids bring new challenges for organizations serving children and youth. Fundamental policy shifts encouraging innovative service approaches are taking place as agencies adjust to the ever-altering needs of the young people and families they serve.

There was a time when youth agencies were seen primarily as places where kids could go to learn and play in safety and to have fun, while parents carried on the important business of working to put a roof over their family's heads and food on their table. While this agency role remains important, for many of today's families it is no longer enough. Many parents are asking for and expecting more from services to which they entrust their offspring. They are not only interested in what programs are offered for their children but also want to know if and how their children will be able to integrate this learning into their lives, an important step toward them achieving their full potential.

Beginning at daycare facilities for very young children, parents seek to know if and how they can deploy some of the well-defined and tested agency approaches into their own daily relations with their sons and daughters. And many agencies are finding that although parent involvement and education can be challenging, when done well it offers unprecedented opportunity for organizations to expand their positive influence on children far beyond a particular facility, program, or activity.

Organizations that have proactively sought parental engagement have learned that parents today are seeking out agencies that encourage and support their parenting experience. They want family activities, frequent contact and updates, and community-based parent education opportunities that focus on helping them improve their parenting skills. Today's parents desire—and some demand—to be a central part of an agency's influence in their child's life. In response, many progressive children/youth organizations are enthusiastically supporting increased parental interest and involvement. Some are going one step further. They are soliciting, encouraging, and facilitating the participation of parents.

Since about the year 2000, I have had opportunity to spend untold hours with audiences comprising thousands of parents, young people, educators, teachers, business leaders, recreation professionals, and minor sports leaders, among many others. What I have heard from them consistently speaks to the heightened expectations they have of those they select to offer programs and activities to young people today.

As a parent, insist that an agency satisfactorily answer the question "Why do you do what you do?" Their answers will help you judge the relevance of their program offerings to your youngster. Most credible agencies confirm that their program staff and volunteers are required to participate in training, accreditation, and certification that is appropriate and often legally required for many activities today. Ask about criminal record checks and look for evidence that program policies are continually updated and rigorously applied. Here are some random suggestions that may guide you in determining what to look for.

Learning to Manage Expectations

During the many years I worked within the voluntary youth/family service sector across Canada, program evaluation by organizations (and sometimes by an outside agency) aimed to answer the following question: "Are we doing things right?" Simply stated, do the activities and programs we offer meet or exceed acceptable industry standards within the recreational/social services sector in which we are mandated? Do we meet the standard of assuring safe passage of children throughout the services we offer?

Today, an additional, more relevant question is often being asked—and it is remarkably different. The question "Are we doing things right?" has in addition become "Are we doing the right things?" Are we as an organization or agency offering services, activities, relationships, and challenges that meet or exceed the needs and expectations of today's children, youth, their families, and the funders who ultimately determine if and what services we offer.

If an organization's self-evaluation reveals it is doing the unnecessary, the less important, or, at worst, the wrong things, it does not much matter that they are doing these things well. What matters is that they find ways of engaging all of their stakeholders, from program participants to board members, in identifying and implementing enlightened programs and activities that are the "right service responses" to meet the needs of those they serve, while of course they continue "to do things right."

Today's parents are not inclined to accept glib and imprecise agency answers to questions such as "What do you offer children who participate in your activities?" They are not going to be satisfied with vague responses along the lines of "We build character and self-esteem, we encourage social interaction and build self-confidence in kids," or that less frequently but sadly still offered rationale, "We keep kids off the streets." To which, by the way, parents have been known to respond, "So do shopping centres."

Today's parents demand real answers and evidence-based results. "Now, tell me *why* you do it?" they may insist. "What difference do you really make, and how will you accomplish these important expectations I have?" As I hope I am making clear, providing effective service to children and young people today is not about slogans, well-intentioned yet unfocused leadership, or woolly mission statements. It is about delivering enlightened, growth-enhancing opportunities with measurable outcomes so that organizations, parents, and young people themselves are more likely to walk away knowing children's needs and potential have been acknowledged and addressed. By taking more analytical approaches to program selection, parents are playing a more active role in guiding the way youth-serving organizations offer their important services.

For many youth agencies, sports organizations, and other youth programs and activities, this increasingly better-informed consumer appraisal has led to a paradigm shift in how they design, deploy, evaluate, and justify their program offerings. This positive agency response to parent input has given new significance to parent-agency partnerships, which are becoming the gold standard for service development.

Simon Sinek's Golden Circle

This chapter opened with a quote from Simon Sinek, who teaches graduate-level strategic communications at Columbia University. Sinek has been described as "a visionary thinker with a rare intellect, who teaches leaders and organizations how to inspire people." His book *Start with Why: How Great Leaders Inspire Everyone to Take Action* delves into a naturally occurring pattern of human decision making that explains why we are inspired by some people, leaders, messages, and organizations over others. A simple explanation of his approach is represented in the diagram below, which he calls the Golden Circle.

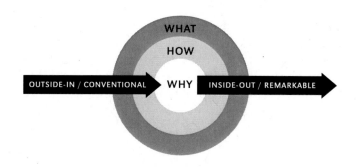

Sinek's concept of the Golden Circle has direct relevance to organizations serving youth. It suggests that such agencies must understand the motivations of future members and clients. These "customers" are less likely to engage a service based on WHAT your service is. Nor are they likely to be persuaded by an explanation of HOW you will meet their needs. Instead, they will increasingly make that important choice of whether or not to engage a service based on your explanation of WHY you do it and the beliefs that led you to choose your current course of action.

From a parental viewpoint, Sinek's theory has practical applications. It is a magic formula that can help us to dig deeper to determine the "why" behind services that agencies offer our children. At the same time, it offers the opportunity for a major rethinking of the way in which agencies serving youth justify and design the services and programs they offer to us and our children.

Throughout this book I have emphasized Search Institute's Developmental Assets research and approach, one model that can explain an agency's motivation for selecting the service goals it prioritizes. For example, let me take Asset 8, Youth as resources— Young people are given useful roles in the community. Here is what I would look for in an agency purporting to promote this value in young people:

- Written explanations of why they promote their youth programs, activities, and leadership development services for members.

- Evidence of formal staff selection and training that ensures all staff and volunteers are given opportunity to develop, teach, and practise age-appropriate leadership skills.

- A formal ongoing Junior Leadership development component wherever appropriate in the design of all services. Open to all members, this program will serve to reaffirm an understanding that the agency's important leadership development/community service goals cannot be met without maximum youth participation.

- Assistant coaching positions, counsellor-in-training roles, and peer counselling programs designed to encourage and sustain experiences where children learn and practise caring for others.

- Intergenerational services given a high priority that draw together children, teens, parents, seniors, and the business community in ways designed to reinforce the belief that young people are indeed an essential part of the solution … not the problem.

Worldwide adoption by youth agencies of this Asset Approach offers further evidence of its potential to effectively measure, backed by research, an agency's ability to deliver the learning opportunities and engagement they feel are important to the development of healthy, responsible young people. Throughout North America over the past twenty or more years, many YM/YMCAS, Boys and Girls Clubs, Big Brothers and Big Sisters organizations, Parks and Recreation departments, Lions Quest Canada, child care services, schools, police services, and government child and youth services have already adopted the Asset Approach. It compels them to examine and respond to the "why?" question. It asks agencies to offer tangible evidence that their programs are more likely to produce the measurable outcomes parents rightly seek from services important in the lives of their children and young people.

Besides youth service organizations, others using the Asset Approach include law enforcement agencies—the subject of the next chapter.

LESSONS TO TAKE AWAY

1. Parents today expect youth agencies to provide more than "babysitting" services. They want to be involved and seek to understand the benefits of programs.

2. Organizations serving children and youth are challenged to manage parental expectations, engage all stakeholders, and provide appropriate services to meet clients' needs.

3. Simon Sinek's concept of the Golden Circle can help both parents and youth service organizations better appreciate the "why" behind service offerings, and the Asset Approach provides one excellent foundation for selecting and evaluating agency programs.

Chapter 9

"Start! In the Name of the Law"

Every society gets the kind of criminal it deserves.
What is equally true is that every community
gets the kind of law enforcement it insists on.
—ROBERT F. KENNEDY, FORMER U.S. SENATOR

DEPENDING ON YOUR PERCEPTIONS of law enforcement, the information in this chapter may surprise you. It concerns Canadian police officers running around our communities trying to catch kids doing something right—yes, you heard me, "right." And believe it or not, they are doing it every day.

You may have already heard the old Lakota tribal saying "When the horse upon which you're riding dies, it may be an appropriate time to dismount." Perhaps the best way for me to start this chapter is with a real-life account of one police officer's experience in applying this Lakota wisdom to modern-day policing. It was about 1998 when RCMP Supt. Ward Clapham, newly appointed as commanding officer of the detachment in Richmond, B.C. (pop. 190,500), told me of an earlier experience he had had as detachment commander in Vermilion, a small rural community (pop. 4,472) east of Edmonton. There he had a discouraging first visit to an elementary school in his new community. It constituted a worrying reality check as to how eight- and nine-year-old children perceived police officers in their town.

With permission from the students' teacher, he had handed each child a blank piece of paper and asked them to draw a picture of what a police officer looked like to them. Within five minutes, artwork began to pile up next to him on the corner of the teacher's desk at the front of the room. Without exception, each drawing contained an image of the head of a police officer, complete with a stern look on his/her face, each face framed in the window of a patrol car. Vermilion's children were telling the detachment's new commanding officer that their perception of RCMP officers was one of men and women with an angry look on their faces while peering out the window of a police car.

Superintendent Clapham told me that for him, those children's drawings precipitated an important reality check. He realized that the respect and cooperation given cops by kids would mirror the respect shown them by police officers. It would be relationships—not mandate—that would bring and keep kids onside with the law. Clapham concluded that when it came to relating effectively with children and young people, police officers like him had been riding a dead horse for too long. He determined that the negative perception of the force had to change if the police were to ever be successful in reducing the rising rates of crime and vandalism among the young people in their community.

So it was that a seemingly routine classroom visit in Vermilion many years ago eventually spawned a movement called *positive ticketing*, a community program where police officers "catch kids doing something right" and reward them with a voucher to some free fun or activity. This program was to change forever the approach and effectiveness of many police officers throughout the world, who today understand and act upon their belief that the best way to reduce crime is to prevent it from happening in the first place.

The notion of cops "catching kids doing something right" was born in Richmond, B.C., when a newly appointed RCMP commanding officer recognized that something wasn't working and had to be fixed. Ward Clapham's excellent book entitled *Breaking with the Law* describes the program's impressive results. In 2001, the first year after the program was instituted, the Richmond detachment was handing out 25,000 positive tickets a year (a 3–1 ratio compared to violations). Youth-related complaint calls eventually dropped by over 60 percent, keeping more than one thousand youth out of trouble with the law.

Positive tickets became a gateway leading to better police-youth relationships and increased respect. Initial attempts at determining the number of young people redeeming the tickets were abandoned when police learned that many kids chose to keep their tickets as a memento or "trophy" of their positive contact with cops. Here is how Clapham explains the program and its benefits:

> The program is based on the simple philosophy that recognizing and rewarding good behavior will inspire and motivate greater good behavior. Positive Tickets are used as the vehicle to make a connection and build trusting relationships with youth. The principles of this innovative approach have been proven to significantly reduce juvenile problems in a community, boost self-esteem and morale, improve community relations with youth, and lower juvenile crime costs.

And read Clapham's summary of what for him personally is the greatest reward of positive tickets.

> The part that makes it worthwhile is pulling into a parking lot full of kids and instead of running away from me, they swarm me. The rewarding part is driving down the street, looking out my window at some kids, and having them wave at me. The real result is seeing a youth who was on the edge of crime now

far from it because he or she made a friend with one of my officers through Positive Tickets. The payoff is that kids don't feel
I'm hunting them anymore. They see me as a friend.

Police recognized from the beginning of program implemen-
tation that the challenge of unacceptable youth crime and conduct in a community is never simply a policing problem. RCMP
leadership in Richmond comprehended that no effective and sustained community change would be achieved unless the entire
community recognized and understood the problem and then
became personally involved as part of the solution.

Superintendent Clapham met with his officers and told them
what he had heard and seen and that things had to change. He
did not know exactly how, he was not sure when, but he knew
this change would not happen without the support of every officer in the detachment. And they got the message and chose to
create detachment-wide teams focused on creating new, positive,
and sustained relationships with young people.

Clapham then went to Richmond's mayor and council and
told them that they had to become involved. They too got the
message. In fact, council passed and published a public proclamation declaring their commitment to make Richmond, B.C., the
best place in the world in which children could live and grow.
That proclamation announced the official launch of an ongoing
asset-building initiative that has resulted in police-received com-
plaints related to young people in the community dropping by
over 67 percent between 1998 and 2007.

In 1998, I got involved by conducting the first of what became
a series of over thirty police asset-building training events offered
to every member of the Richmond RCMP detachment. Unprecedented community-wide engagement became the tipping point
in Richmond's asset-building initiative, with police playing a
continuing role as leaders among leaders. A community team as
had never been seen before came together, comprised of young

people along with representatives from city council, the RCMP, the school district, Parks and Recreation, voluntary agencies, the regional health authority, business, service clubs, and senior citizens groups. All embraced the single goal of acknowledging and building on the strengths of the community's youth.

The resulting so-called Asset Cabinet became the driving force behind Richmond's asset-building initiative. Participants met informally once a month, never in excess of one hour. There were no minutes, no Robert's Rules of Order, and no formal agenda, simply a unique group of influential citizens determined to make their community the most asset-rich community in the world, one in which young people could live and grow to healthy adulthood.

It is a model that has been replicated in various forms throughout Canada, the United States, and, in recent years, the world. Police officers saw themselves as equals among equals committed to a common purpose: to assure healthier, safer, more engaged, more respectful, and more respected young people who, with their elders, could live together in safety, peace, harmony, and shared responsibility.

This recap of the Richmond experience is only a bare-bones account. You can learn more of the details by reading Clapham's book *Breaking with the Law: The Story of Positive Tickets.*

One Twelve-Year-Old Boy's Experience with Positive Ticketing

It was indirectly the result of a Richmond police officer catching a boy doing something right that provided my favourite and most compelling evidence of the effectiveness of positive ticketing. Concluding an asset-building workshop for foster parents in the Fraser Valley, east of Vancouver, around 2006, I had just finished showing the Richmond positive ticketing video when a foster mom in the audience stood up and said, "Oh, Keith! I know all about positive tickets." When I learned she did not live in Richmond, I asked how she had heard about the idea. Her story is one I will always remember.

She explained that she had once lived in Richmond and became aware of the positive ticketing idea while undertaking a weekly cleanup of her twelve-year-old foster son's bedroom. On his bulletin board she noticed a ticket from the Richmond RCMP. At dinner that night she could not resist. "Andrew," she said, "I was cleaning your room and noticed you got a ticket from the police. What's going on?" That prompted Andrew to offer the kind of minimal response kids are famous for when asked to explain the unexplainable. "Oh, it was really nothing, Mom!" Like most parents, his foster mom persisted and the story unfolded.

He explained: "Remember last week you asked me to go to the corner store to pick up a few groceries? As I walked along Westminster Avenue to the store, there was a mother pushing a stroller with a baby in it, with a little boy holding on to the side. For some reason, the little boy let go of the stroller and started running out between two parked cars and right onto the street. I knew something bad could happen to him so I ran out, grabbed his arm, and brought him back and reattached him to the stroller.

"Just as I did that, a police car pulled up at an angle against the curb with his red and blue lights flashing. I thought I was going to get picked up for kidnapping. Then this big policeman got out of his car, came over to me, kneeled down on the sidewalk, and asked me my name and age. I told him, 'My name's Andrew and I'm twelve years old.'

"He said, 'Andrew, I just saw you do one of the smartest, bravest things I have ever seen a young man do in our community. If you hadn't grabbed that little boy before he got out into the traffic, he could have been seriously hurt or maybe killed. Can I give you a ticket to remind you how important kids like you are in our community?'

"He went on, 'So that's how I got the ticket, Mom—from a cop who told me he was proud of what I did.' "

The story did not end there. The foster mom went on to explain that a week later she was in the same bedroom cleaning up a familiar mess when she looked over and saw that the ticket remained on the notice board. She took the time to read the back of the ticket. It gave Andrew a free pass to go swimming, play pitch-and-putt golf, and get a free slice of pizza and a pop. At dinner, she broached the subject again. "Andrew," she said, "I noticed you haven't used your ticket yet. How come?"

The boy replied, "Mom, I'll never use that ticket. You see, it's proof a cop thinks I'm a good kid."

More Cops Doing the Right Thing by Building Assets

The foster mother's story reminds me, as well, of Insp. Warren Dosko, commanding officer of the RCMP detachment in St. Albert, Alberta (pop. 61,000). From 2007, when he was named officer in charge, Inspector Dosko rallied city council, young people, social services, schools, and the business community, among others, to create one of the most high-profile youth-led asset-building initiatives in Canada. A City of St. Albert webpage entitled "Assets at Work" reads in part:

> Asset building requires the entire community's help. Parents, children, teachers, neighbours and community and business leaders—we all have a role to play in ensuring St. Albert youth have what they need to achieve personal success and lead healthy lives.

The page also features the smiling faces of eight young community members, linked to "stories … about St. Albertans doing their part to make a difference in the lives of youth." You can read those stories at www.stalbert.ca/assets-at-work.

Notably, this is the third Canadian community in which Dosko has spearheaded a community-wide asset initiative. In both Princeton and 100 Mile House, B.C., positive approaches with children and young people are rooted in this remarkable officer's success in achieving intergenerational understanding, respect, and involvement. Meanwhile, in Delta, B.C., a largely rural community (pop. 103,000) next door to Richmond, Chief Jim Cessford advocates asset building as an important police tactic and practises the approach himself with the minor baseball and hockey teams he coaches in his free time.

And B.C. is not the only province adopting the Asset Approach. When you first take a glance at the EKC initiative in Brockville, Ontario, you learn that the anagram stands for Every Kid Counts. The initiative began when Chief Barry King of the Brockville Police Service saw the need for a major and coordinated approach to improve disintegrating relationships between his community and its young people. The asset-based approach the community chose now involves forty public and non-profit agencies who together have created a sustained strength-based network aimed at touching the lives of every child, young person, and family in their community.

That same Chief Barry King successfully obtained the endorsement of the Canadian Association of Chiefs of Police, which led to closer association between asset builders and the North American Safe Communities movement. Safe Communities Canada is a national charitable organization. According to its website, the organization is "dedicated to helping communities across the country build the capacity and resources they will need as they commit to mounting coordinated, collaborative programmes designed to reduce the pain and cost of injury and promote a culture of safety for all their citizens."

As Supt. Ward Clapham of Richmond knew—and most parents would concur—it is essential that kids have a positive image of police officers. Positive ticketing can help to create and reinforce this view. The positive ticketing approach is being constantly modified and practised in schools, daycare programs, minor sports organizations, families, and youth recreation and treatment programs.

The next chapter discusses other trusted professionals who come into even more frequent contact with our children—their teachers.

LESSONS TO TAKE AWAY

1. Positive ticketing, a police-led program where officers "catch kids doing something right," is being used to build relationships and ultimately reduce juvenile crime and vandalism.

2. Asset-building initiatives have maximum effect when all members of a community are involved in the effort to build on the strengths of their young people.

3. Such initiatives can be started by law enforcement agencies, local governments, school districts or principals, non-profit organizations—or even youth themselves.

Chapter 10

The New Three Rs
of Education

> *There is an old saying that the course of*
> *civilization is a race between catastrophe*
> *and education. In a democracy like ours, we*
> *must be sure that education wins the race.*
> —JOHN F. KENNEDY

MUCH OF OUR CHILDREN'S out-of-home time is spent in a classroom or participating in activities led by teachers. These educators make an irreplaceable difference in our kids' lives every day. I know this from personal experience of how teachers influenced my own life. You read about one of those teachers in chapter 1. There were more, too numerous to name. And their influence did not always take place in the classroom, but they intuitively understood and taught the new three Rs referred to in the title of this chapter.

- *Relationships.* Every boy and girl needs these in order to grow and achieve their potential in life. All great teachers help kids build and sustain healthy relationships.

- *Respect.* Children's respect for themselves and others comes from experiencing respect from people important in their lives. Teachers know children are important and act accordingly.

- *Responsibility.* Children first learn to be responsible through the role modelling of people significant to them. Teachers give young people age-appropriate tasks, challenges, and guidelines that move them toward responsible behaviour.

I learned from and came to admire industrial art teachers who worked evenings alongside kids building sets for school plays, physical education teachers who coached evening and weekend games and practices, music teachers who conducted band practices and concerts, and countless others who spent hours tutoring, listening to, and encouraging kids who sought extra time and attention outside of regular teaching hours. All of these activities required teachers' personal time, energy, and sometimes infinite patience.

As a kid it never occurred to me that teachers did not get paid for extracurricular activities; I thought they were there just because it was what teachers did. Come to think of it, I did not meet one teacher who seemed drawn to teaching by the opportunity to develop curricula, supervise detention, write tedious reports, or attend what I always assumed were fairly boring staff meetings, which in my era I imagined took place in smoke-filled rooms. No, this kid's perception was that teachers were there because they wanted to give us the tools we needed to be successful in life. That is why they became teachers.

And then my own sons and daughter entered Grade 1 for what I hoped would be at least twelve years of teachers in their futures, and for the most part their educational experience was overwhelmingly positive. Then came the grandchildren, whose academic pursuits one observes from a greater distance, but the impact of good teachers was still there, in my case in two different countries: passionate, bright, caring, talented, and often humorous adults finding ways to make a personal connection with a mosaic of students, into whose lives they introduced knowledge, ideas, challenge, and confidence every school day of the year, rain or shine.

Without question, most parents appreciate and respect good teachers. Then why is it that so often parent-teacher communications end up focusing primarily on what's *wrong* rather than on what is often remarkably *right*—and encouraging—about our children's school experience? While acknowledging and dealing with poor performance in school is important in order for children to achieve their academic potential, how does a parent give equal or greater recognition to what teachers and our children are doing well? Seems to me the following "assets" should be indicated on report cards: making friends, being honest and reliable, displaying tolerance and understanding to others, being cooperative, accepting leadership roles.

For those of you whose school experiences were mainly positive, one of the best ways to better understand your child's school experience is to reflect on your own time in school. When the subject of great teachers arises among my circle of friends, talk inevitably and quickly turns to the most memorable teachers in our lives. Not surprisingly, most often we find ourselves talking about the ones who were most demanding of us to meet our potential, who were not easily—or ever—hoodwinked by our "dog ate my homework" explanations, whose assignments somehow always got completed, and who found ways of influencing us to want to be like them.

Such reflections may also remind us that, as it is with parents, not all teachers are equal in terms of commitment, knowledge, or passion to teach. Be that as it may, we are in this together, and nothing trumps the needs and expectations of our children. Maybe it is time we began building more effective partnerships with teachers and became increasingly involved in a constructive way. Perhaps we should refocus on being appreciative as well as vigilant of our children's teachers, on giving equal or greater time to celebrate and support the vast majority of educators who every day make our lives better.

On the remote chance there are some skeptics out there who think I give teachers too much credit, rest assured, I never have and never will be an accredited member of the teaching profession—just someone who acknowledges he would not be who and where he is if untold teachers had not taken the time to become significant in his life.

Social Justice in the Classroom

This discussion of teachers leads me to a more general observation about some of the changes in education over the years, most of them for the better. There are far too many positive changes to list in this short chapter, but this topic is one that impinges on the core theme of this book: finding ways every day to more intentionally give all kids what they need to succeed in life.

When I was a kid going to school, the whole notion of social justice and social responsibility was not a topic of frequent conversations. In fact, I don't even remember hearing the terms. Not among the kids I knew, nor between us and our teachers. This is not to say we weren't learning about these issues, but we learned about them passively through good people living their lives and "doing the right thing."

Fortunately today, the teaching of these important life understandings and values has become more formalized. Subjects such as discrimination, diversity, human rights, oppression, ethics, and values are increasingly taught and discussed in classroom settings, where they form part of the curriculum. Inequity, poverty, and social injustice are faced head-on and talked about as they should be. Not only are kids learning the facts and theories of social justice, they are being given opportunities to put this knowledge into practice at school, with their families, and in their community. My friends, this is big stuff.

The story that follows illustrates how students in one high school responded to teacher-inspired opportunities for them to acknowledge and act on their ability to make a difference in the lives of others.

Progressive School Policies in Penticton

In 2010 I visited the Princess Margaret Secondary School in Penticton, British Columbia. Principal Don MacIntyre and I had participated in some asset-building training together, and Princess Margaret was one of numerous Skaha School District schools in B.C.'s Okanagan Valley to pioneer education-based asset building in Canada. I was interested see to how MacIntyre had introduced the Asset Approach into a school culture—how he made the idea come alive in a setting in which all students would be immersed in strength-based learning. Above all, I wondered how he had created a school environment in which every student came to believe they were part of the solution, not the problem.

My first impression of that visit remains fresh in my mind. I had to park my car a block and a half away from the main entrance. As I walked along the sidewalk toward the school, I met somewhere between ten and fifteen students, taking a break between classes, simply walking, or engaged informally in outdoor activity. Without exception, every student I met looked up as they passed by, established eye contact, slowed their gait, and greeted me with a friendly hello. One young guy even high-fived me. This was unprecedented for me, and before I got to the front door I realized I was about to enter a school that was doing something differently.

I will not go on at length about what I learned from those students' principal, but several of the ideas he described were a revelation to me. Encouragingly, over the past couple of years in my work with K–12 schools, I have seen growing evidence that the teaching, modelling, and practising of behaviours that encourage and instill qualities of fairness, tolerance, and everyday kindness in young people are becoming a recognized and growing priority.

Take a moment and place yourself in the sneakers of a young student passing through the door of this Penticton high school for the first time. Imagine walking into a school where every student is assigned a teacher observer/mentor responsible to monitor them and assure their safe passage throughout the year. Here is a school that has taken technology and used it to their advantage. If you as a student are absent from Princess Margaret Secondary, you will probably get a text message telling you that you have been missed and asking if you need any help. When you attend your first orientation on the first day of the school year, you will find yourself spending half a day talking about social responsibility, politeness, and other important social skills—values such as fairness, honesty, and respect—as well as the novel policy: no student ever fails at this school. As the principal told me, "We don't do failure here. Every student is good at something."

Teddy Stoddard's Favourite Teacher

That comment by an extraordinary high school principal reminded me of the story given to me by a retired schoolteacher many years ago. At the end of a midwinter evening workshop I was leading in a small, snow-laden mountain town in central British Columbia, she approached and asked if I would wait for twenty minutes while she walked home to retrieve a story of unknown origin that she felt best depicted what can only be offered by a sensitive, dedicated, and passionate teacher. To this day, over a quarter of a century later, I have had no reason to question her determination, and I owe that anonymous educator for a depiction of teachers that has motivated thousands. I can think of no more appropriate and compelling story to conclude this chapter—appropriate and compelling because it holds potential to remind us of the vast majority of teachers in our lives who made a difference. And sometimes, just sometimes, who led us to strive to be just like them. Be forewarned: it's a story that can evoke powerful personal reflections in those lucky enough to have had a Mrs. Thompson in their life.

How a Rhinestone Bracelet, ¼ Bottle of Perfume, a Caring Teacher, and a Sullen Little Boy Made a Difference!

There is a story told many years of an elementary teacher. Her name was Mrs. Jean Thompson. As she stood in front of her fifth-grade class on the very first day of school, she told the children a lie. Like most teachers, she looked at her students and said that she loved each of them the same. But that was impossible, because there in the front row, slumped in his seat, was a little boy named Teddy Stoddard. Mrs. Thompson had watched Teddy the year before and noticed that he didn't play well with the other children, that his clothes were messy, and that he constantly needed a bath. And Teddy could be quite unpleasant.

It got to the point where Mrs. Thompson would actually take delight in marking his papers with a broad red pen, making bold X's and then putting a big "F" at the top of his paper. At the school where Mrs. Thompson taught, she was required to review each child's records and she put Teddy's off until last.

However, when she reviewed his file, she was surprised and saddened.

Teddy's first-grade teacher wrote: "Teddy is a bright child with a ready laugh. He does his work neatly and has good manners. He is a joy to be around."

His second-grade teacher wrote: "Teddy is an excellent student, well liked by his classmates, but he is troubled because his mother has a terminal illness and life at home must be a struggle."

His third-grade teacher wrote: "His mother's death has been hard on him. He tries to do his best but his father doesn't show much interest and his home life will soon affect him if some steps aren't taken."

Teddy's fourth-grade teacher had commented, "Teddy is withdrawn and doesn't show much interest in school. He doesn't have many friends and sometimes sleeps in class. He is frequently tardy and could become a more serious problem."

By now Mrs. Thompson realized the problem and she was ashamed of herself. She felt even worse when her students brought her Christmas presents, wrapped in beautiful ribbons and bright paper, except for Teddy's. His present was clumsily wrapped in the heavy, brown paper that he got from a grocery bag. Mrs. Thompson took pains to open it in the middle of the other presents. Some of the children started to laugh when she found a rhinestone bracelet with some of the stones missing, and a bottle that was one-quarter full of perfume. But she stifled the children's laughter when she exclaimed how pretty the bracelet was, putting it on, and dabbing some of the perfume on her wrist.

Teddy Stoddard stayed after school that day just long enough to say, "Mrs. Thompson, today you smelled just like my mom used to."

After the children left, she cried for at least an hour. On that very day, she quit teaching reading, and writing, and arithmetic. Instead, she began to teach children.

Mrs. Thompson paid particular attention to Teddy. As she worked with him, his mind seemed to come alive. The more she encouraged him, the faster he responded. By the end of the year, Teddy had become one of the smartest children in the class and, despite her lie that she would love all the children the same, Teddy became one of her teacher's pets.

A year later she found a note under her door, from Teddy, telling her that she was the best teacher he had ever had in his whole life. Six years went by before another note from Teddy. He then wrote that he had finished high school, third in his class, and she was still the best teacher he had ever had in his whole life. Four years after that, she got another letter saying that while things had been tough at times, he'd stayed with school, had stuck with it and would soon graduate from college with the highest of honours. He assured Mrs. Thompson that she was still the best and favourite teacher he ever had in his whole life. Then four more years passed and yet another letter came. This time he explained that after he got his bachelor's degree he decided to go a little further. The letter explained that she was still the best and favourite teacher he ever had. But now his name was a little longer. The letter was signed, Theodore F. Stoddard, M.D.

And the story doesn't end there. You see, there was yet another letter that spring. Teddy said he'd met this girl and was going to be married. He explained that his father had died a couple of years ago and he was wondering if Mrs. Thompson might agree to sit in the place at the wedding that was usually reserved for the mother of the groom. Of course, Mrs. Thompson did. And guess what? She wore that bracelet, the one with several rhinestones missing. And she made sure she was wearing the perfume that Teddy remembered his mother wearing on their last Christmas together.

They hugged each other, and Dr. Stoddard whispered In Mrs. Thompson's ear. "Thank you, Mrs. Thompson, for believing in me. Thank you so much for making me feel important and showing me that I could make a difference."

With tears in her eyes, Mrs. Thompson whispered back, "Teddy, you have it all wrong! I didn't know how to teach until I met you."

In the chapter to follow you will learn about how First Nations elders, families, and their young people came together to refocus on *their* traditional values of respect, tolerance, and compassion.

LESSONS TO TAKE AWAY

1. Students, parents, and hence we as a society benefit from knowledgeable, dedicated teachers, who deserve our support and appreciation.

2. If we as a society are to achieve social justice and fairness, young people need to sense, experience, and practise these values 24/7 in all segments of their lives—at school, at home, in community programs, and above all in their daily interaction with the important adults in their lives.

3. One progressive high school in Penticton, B.C., illustrates the supportive, respectful atmosphere that can develop when the Asset Approach underpins school policies.

Chapter 11

What the Secwepemc People Taught Me

Like a dream catcher, Developmental Assets are the
supporting threads in a young person's life that
can keep them away from harm and invite goodness
—Excerpted from Helping Kids
Succeed—Alaskan Style

A T THE INVITATION of the Q'wemtsín Health Society, I had the opportunity a while ago to spend a memorable day with approximately one hundred young people and their families from among the seventeen bands who comprise the Secwepemc Nation. They live throughout the interior of British Columbia, the newest generation of a people who have lived in their traditional Shuswap territory for at least ten thousand years. They wanted to learn how they could more effectively encourage their young people to achieve their potential and, at this particular event, talk specifically about reducing the alarming rate of suicide among First Nation teens. Ironically, rather than focusing on everything that might be going wrong, we found ourselves enthusiastically sharing the potential for all of us to make things go right!

I was welcomed into a gathering of remarkable Aboriginal parents, children, young people, grandparents, and community leaders who quietly shared with me their deeply held love, enthusiasm, wisdom, devotion, and concern for their children. In the course of the time we spent together that day, we engaged in an animated intergenerational conversation about how they were giving and could increasingly give their kids what they needed to succeed in life.

The day began with recognition that Canadian Aboriginal people have throughout their history understood the essential and important role parents and elders must play in the development of future generations. We agreed we have the greatest impact on our children when we occasionally revisit our challenges and, more importantly, act on the realities we find—when we answer the question "What are each of us willing and able to do personally to help shape healthy attitudes and behaviour among the young people we influence?"

In opening the event as a workshop facilitator, I read the following excerpt from the publication *Helping Kids Succeed— Alaskan Style.*

> What is the asset framework? We usually think of assets as money or possessions. Their value grows over time. We can use them in many ways. And the more of them we collect, the more secure we feel. The same is true of the assets described in this book—youth developmental assets!

I told the group we are simply talking about important life building blocks in children's lives that help them grow up to be strong, capable, and caring adults. The Asset Approach offers a model that takes us one practical step further and describes what we can do personally to inspire our kids to succeed. As outlined in chapter 5, the model is a helpful road map designed to help us take appropriate steps every day toward ensuring that our children acquire the experience and confidence so critical to their healthy development.

At this Sun Peaks workshop we talked about the notion of resiliency: about equipping our young people to be able to face challenges with confidence; to bounce back from disappointment, hardship, and failure; and sometimes, to grow and thrive through adversity. We agreed that the most resilient kids cope with stressful things in life in a way that helps them become stronger as a result, as they often acquire important new coping skills. And many kids derive their responses to stress through watching how the adults in their lives cope with setbacks and disappointments.

I shared an important First Nation story from Alaska, a true story that told of a happening in a small community of six hundred mainly Aboriginal people, many of whom had gathered to speak of their concern for their children and youth and the possibility of introducing the Asset Approach into their lives. The village, reached only by plane or boat, remained isolated much of the year, with residents making a living mostly by commercial and subsistence fishing. The presenter that night had been talking for about forty minutes when he noticed an elder sitting in the back of the room.

The elder stood and began moving empty chairs to make more space for himself. "For years," he explained, "we have been trying to tell people that we need to focus on the strengths of our communities, the strengths of our traditions, and the strengths of ourselves. These are the things that we focused on a long time ago, and we've been waiting for seventy-five years for these things to be focused on again.

"I am a fisherman," he continued. "Fishermen have a common understanding. When we are out fishing, if the boat should get a hole in it, we know we must act quickly. If we are in sight of land, we must try to slow the leak and make a run for the harbour, where we can safely work to repair the damage. However, if we are far out of sight of the land, we know that we must repair the damage because we have little hope of making it to safety.

"When it comes to our children and the health of our communities, we are far, far out to sea and out of sight of land. Now is the time to use these ideas to fix the holes in our boats and allow us to carry all of our children and our children's children to safety. Whatever we want from young people, we must first of all give them." The elder returned to his seat and motioned for the presenter to continue.

After hearing this story, the people of the Secwepemc Nation spent the next few hours talking, sharing, and encouraging one another to consider what each of them could give their children so they were more likely to experience a safer, happier, more responsible and fulfilled adulthood. I quickly realized that in a space of time measured in minutes, my role had shifted from one of an imported expert to that of mutual learner. Here is some of what I learned in our day and a half together.

A Circle of Laughter and Caring

On the evening prior to the workshop, I was invited to experience Native drumming and the playing of traditional Aboriginal games. The cast included participants ranging from seven to seventy years. Young children, teenagers, and elders participated as equals with a passion, humour, dignity, and sense of caring I have seldom seen in intergenerational events.

If you ever see, and really hear as I did for the first time, the sometimes haunting significance of Native drumming and chanting, you can be drawn toward a better understanding of First Nations' passion for life, sharing, and caring, their reverence for the environment, and their love of their children.

As mentioned, I also watched for the first time the playing of one of their traditional games. Honestly, the bone game of Lahal remains a continuing enigma to this first-time-watching white man. It is a blend of drumming, chanting, challenge, mystery, fun, complexity, laughter, patience, and respect. After all, how many games end with every single participant moving slowly through a circle shaking hands or high-fiving each other and thanking them for their time and sportsmanship?

I learned that Native children are first and foremost loved and cherished, not only by their parents but also by significant others who work hard at creating that mythical village we hear so much about—the one we are told is imperative to the raising of healthy, responsible, and caring kids. I was reminded that for many First Nation families, money is not the measure to be used in determining how healthy children are nourished, raised, and supported. Love, spoken and given freely and frequently, is a powerful substitute.

I was reminded that the greatest challenge for those of us who desire and work to be significant positive influences in children's lives is to acknowledge the simple truth that our young people gather 20 percent of what they get from us based on our words. The other 80 percent they learn from watching our behaviour. First Nation people understand and are working hard to address the challenge of becoming effective mentors, role models, and shapers of young minds.

Translating Talk to Action Steps

Like many attendees at events I facilitate, the Secwepemc people took the opportunity to put to paper some of their thoughts about the workshop. Specifically, they recorded what they planned to do personally to translate "asset talk" into life-changing action when they returned to the children and young people in their families, reserves, villages, neighbourhoods, schools, and lives. You may find something familiar and instructive in what they had to say.

- I'm going to listen to youth more and lecture them less ... just help out more ... very good stories ... listen more—talk less ...

- As a teenager I'm going talk to lonely kids in my school—tell my parents about what I'm learning—talk more with family instead of holding back.

- I plan to communicate with my kids more. Make more time and spend more time with them. Listen to them— it's very important—having family here was a positive experience for us. Thanks.

- I intend to get involved more with developing activities and programs and encouraging youth and child involvement.

- We should extend invitations to parents and caregivers to get involved.

- I will try and put forward ideas in which communities can come together and encourage each other—very good ideas!—Cool!—Do more of these workshops.

- Have one day of fun stuff for family. I learned about things to do together. Wicked!

- What will work for me I will use—excellent presentation—good workshop.

- Too many things I'll do differently to list ... It was fun!

- I'll take all I learned home with me. It was really cool. I'll be more open to all children. Listen to their ideas because what they have to say is important!—Have younger children more involved—share it with my family.—Include everyone of all ages in Assets.

- One day at a time will make a big difference for both me and my children. As a father I will be a good person and a good leader with the help of my kids, friends and family.

Many thanks, my Secwepemc friends. You taught me a lot.

In the next chapter you will learn how the community of Summerland, B.C., has created enhanced levels of intergenerational understanding, respect, and cooperation among their young people, adults, and particularly senior citizens.

LESSONS TO TAKE AWAY

1. Members of the Secwepemc First Nation in B.C.'s interior understand that alarming rates of suicide among their young people will be most effectively addressed when the adults in their lives take time every day to model behaviours that give their kids hope, guidance, and positive direction.

2. They understand and share a belief in the words expressed by an Aboriginal elder in Alaska, "Whatever we want from young people, we must first of all give them." It is an Aboriginal tradition to bestow honour and prestige on elders, who hold in their hands the capacity to guide young people toward a happy, responsible, and fulfilled adulthood.

3. In an evening of traditional drumming and game playing, my hosts in Kamloops demonstrated the intergenerational respect and love that is a vital hallmark of their culture.

Chapter 12

The Summerland
Seniors/Kids Divide

It takes a village to raise a child.
—A FREQUENTLY QUOTED NIGERIAN PROVERB

SOME OF YOU WILL KNOW THE TOWN: a small, bucolic village overlooking Okanagan Lake in the heart of the B.C. Central Interior's fruit-growing and wine-producing area. Visit Summerland (pop. 11,776) in midsummer, or for that matter pretty well any time of the year, and it is easy to be moved to the determination "This is a place I'd like to live, love to raise my family."

In 1998, that was the essence of Summerland as depicted in glossy brochures that greeted sun-addled tourists, who watched in awe as industrious citizens quietly earned their living and lived their lives in apparent harmony. A large percentage of Summerland residents were—and continue to be—senior citizens whose life of hard work has led them to seek the retirement pleasures of this safe, quiet, and scenic destination. It was a Summerland as well made up of growing numbers of young people, many of them teenagers, whose passion in life understandably tended more toward skateboarding, loud music, a need for positive community recognition, and the part-time jobs that would permit them to achieve higher levels of financial independence.

And so it was that citizens of all ages began to sense a tension developing between generations, particularly among teens and the community's senior residents. This tension grew slowly at first but then was felt with an alarming frequency and intensity. Little stuff, admittedly, but not the kind of thing anyone wants to have happening in their community. No one knows whether these tensions started with the kids themselves or with the seniors. But the evidence seemed clear. Seniors did not have a very positive impression of the young people in their community. Maybe you have occasionally heard these kinds of rumblings where you live. "These kids are lazy. Young people today don't have any ambition. They're rude, noisy, and talk and text on their cellphones incessantly. Why don't they get a job?"

In Summerland, seniors did not fare much better in the eyes of young people. Youth observations ran as follows. "They live in gated communities because they don't like us. They don't speak when we meet on the street. They don't show much interest in what we do," and of course the all-encompassing "They don't really care about us."

School leaders and the local RCMP detachment heard and recognized the problem first. The mayor and city council, the Rotary Club, members of the business community, and young people themselves saw it as well. And in what can only be described as the beginning of a miraculous community transformation, this increased awareness and interest resulted in a developing realization that not only was this disconnect between generations real, but that it held potential to harm seniors, harm kids, and reflect poorly on the "community that cares" reputation Summerland had fought hard to build and wanted to retain.

It was at this point in time, in the spring of 1998, that two remarkably timed and then unrelated occurrences led to what some have referred to over the years as the "Summerland Experiment." The first was the introduction by Boys and Girls Clubs of British Columbia of Search Institute's Developmental Assets approach, its first application in Canada. The second "happening" was the arrival on the scene of a remarkable community advocate and champion of young people named Ellen Lloyd, who agreed to accept the leadership role in a fledgling organization that became known as SADI, short for the newly fledged Summerland Asset Development Initiative.

Lloyd's positive response to the city council's invitation to take on the job came with four conditions that she explained were non-negotiable:

1. To the largest extent possible, the initiative would be youth-led, with adults serving in an advisory capacity to leadership drawn from young people within the Summerland community and rural district.

2. The city would provide her with a youth-friendly Mission Control office in City Hall where high-profile youth involvement would offer the public a chance to witness youth leadership in action.

3. No young person would be discouraged from participating. There would be no talk of troubled kids, disadvantaged kids, or delinquent kids. It would be assumed that all young people in Summerland were at-risk and would be treated accordingly.

4. This burgeoning new youth movement must be established and carried out in accordance with the strength-based philosophy of Search Institute of Minneapolis.

In Summerland, the focus would be on what matters to our kids, not on what's the matter with our kids, on introducing and enhancing Developmental Assets in the lives of all young people.

A Comprehensive Survey of Community Youth

As young people began to meet, share ideas, and try to get a handle on the tasks they faced, it became clear that before they could create and deploy any solutions or new approaches, they must first of all identify the challenges. This determination led to the first ever application of Search Institute's Student Profile study in Canada, conducted throughout the entire Summerland school system, in Grades 6 to 12. The study's sole purpose was to determine the number of Developmental Assets present in the lives of Summerland kids.

While many communities utilizing this survey in the past had accepted standard research protocol that suggested a 3 to 5 percent sampling would produce accurate findings, the kids in Summerland decided that was not good enough. Their explanation was compellingly simple: "If just one kid isn't surveyed, then their parents are going to say, 'That's not my kid they're talking about.' " And so it came to pass that the Skaha School District 67, with the blessings of School Superintendent Larry Thomas along with an innovative and enthusiastically supportive high school counsellor, Don Gibbings, gave permission for over one thousand Summerland school students in Grades 6 to 12 to take a full hour of classroom time completing a computer-based, standardized survey instrument, which had already been given to thousands of American young people.

With the anonymity of participating students assured, the survey has since been used to measure the presence of community strengths, weaknesses, and challenges throughout the world. In this instance, the survey was administered not only to young people within the school system, but also to kids involved in street activity and non-traditional educational services. It was again the young people who insisted on this. "After all," they explained, "this is about every kid in Summerland."

Summerland's young people, school administrators, and city council agreed that the results would become the young people's report card back to the community in which they lived. School officials proposed it should be delivered by the very young people who had helped bring it to their schools and had participated in providing the data collected. When results were finally compiled in the winter of 2000, the long-awaited forty-page final report and summary was returned to Summerland for distribution. That Search Institute document, entitled *Developmental Assets: A Profile of the Youth of Summerland—Attitudes and Behaviours*, was to become the foundation of the Summerland Asset Development Initiative.

Young people unanimously agreed to present the findings to the school board and school officials, whose trust and faith in them had made it possible.

As with all student profile studies, the results were mixed. There were plenty of positives: good things that were happening in the community for kids. It was evident these should be acknowledged and expanded. But there were some downers, real downers. For the purposes of this chapter, let me simply mention one. To the question "Do you feel valued and respected by adults in your community outside of your own family?" 20 percent of the young people surveyed said yes, but a full 80 percent answered no. Here was tangible research evidence that what many people in Summerland experienced and sensed was indeed a reality. A troubling disconnect existed between the community's young people and the adults in their lives beyond their own families.

Opening Up the Lines of Communication

The response of school leaders was thoughtful, respectful, and enthusiastic. They determined they would increase and enhance the leadership experiences young people were having in school, particularly the kind that gave students a chance to demonstrate in the community their desire and willingness to make a positive difference. At the same time, school officials recognized many of the challenges revealed through the study would require community-wide understanding and action. Educators encouraged the young people to carry their message to city council, and council responded by inviting them to a full meeting of council to deliver the much-awaited report card on what it was like for kids to live in their community.

That report to council, delivered by four teenagers, was listened to intently and immediately acted upon. In the words of then-mayor Don Cameron, "This is so important, you young people should be telling it to the entire community." The city agreed to sponsor a community-wide public forum where the young people would deliver the results of their survey to anyone in the community who would take the time to listen.

And take the time they did! I attended that forum, convened in a large public facility, and watched in amazement as over three hundred Summerland residents gathered to hear their young people talk about what it was like to grow up in their hometown. The good news, and there was a lot of good news, was welcomed. At the same time, the bad news, and there was some bad news, seemed to come as a shock to many who had gathered, some of them seniors from nearby gated residences.

Fourteen-year-old Carley Julien, one of the by now veteran teen presenters, was tasked that night with delivering the results from students' response to the survey statement that read, "In my neighbourhood there are a lot of people who care about me." She told the assembled audience, "Twenty percent of kids like me and my friends believe you care about us. Eighty percent feel that you don't." The news drew an immediate response from a senior near the front. "Carley, it's not a very good survey. We love you kids." And this straight-talking teen student gave an answer that stands out in my mind still today as evidence of the magnificent kindness and candour kids often display. Here is my recollection of what she said.

"With all respect, ma'am, you sometimes have a funny way of showing it." The senior responded kindly, asking her to explain what she meant. The girl went on. "Anyone who lives in Summerland knows that our high school's located right on Main Street, not far from the post office where many seniors go every day at lunch to pick up their mail. It's at that same time that kids like me and my friends get out of school for lunch hour and walk up and down Main Street drinking a pop or just soaking up the sun. Often when we're walking along the sidewalk we look ahead and see a group of seniors heading our way on the same side of the street.

"Do you know what many of you do?" she asked. Some seniors responded in unison. "Tell us."

"What you do is you look up ahead and see three or four kids walking towards you, and then you do something we don't understand. You actually cross over to the sidewalk on the other side of Main Street until you've passed where we are, and then you cross back and continue to the post office. Why do you do that?"

The same senior who had engaged the teen responded, "We do that, Carley, because we're afraid of teenagers." To which this young lady replied, "Why are you afraid of me? I'm fourteen years old, I've never hurt a thing or person in my life, and I don't have much chance to talk with my grandparents or to people like you. Why are you afraid of me?"

The senior replied, "Carley, we read about the behaviour of kids like you every morning in the paper, and every night on television we see images of the terrible kinds of things kids are doing." That simple exchange, offered kindly and sincerely, was the beginning of an amazing adventure in respectful coexistence among seniors and young people in the town of Summerland that has flourished and carries on in various ways to this day.

As had been predetermined, at the end of that evening, groups comprising a mix of adults, senior citizens, and young people sat down together at tables throughout the meeting hall. Their task was straightforward and clear: talk about how they could break down these misunderstandings and barriers among the adults and young people of their community. The role assigned me by the young people that night was also clear: to serve as a neutral, non-resident observer and to be available if called upon to answer audience questions specific to Search Institute's Developmental Assets.

All Kids Are Our Kids. A Community's Response.

At the table I happened to be at, I listened to Carley and adults from all walks of life begin to calmly share their feelings and ideas. I was particularly moved by a florist who explained he had a shop on Main Street and that most of his customers were seniors. He opened his contribution by telling Carley that the survey was absolutely right, that every day he heard seniors talking about and dwelling on the negative behaviour of kids in their community.

He went on to explain to the teens present that he had an idea. He told them that every Thursday he had a dozen or so carnations or roses left over that he could not sell. His suggestion: "Why don't you kids come by after school on Thursday and pick up a few roses or carnations and walk up and down Main Street handing them out to seniors and asking if they'll take the time to talk with you about making things better in our community?"

Not surprisingly, the kids thought it was a great idea. After all, what better way to cadge the odd pop or coffee and maybe even talk to some interesting people? When the kids who had picked up the flowers that first day did not return to his store by closing time to report on what they had learned, the florist was somewhat disappointed, but consoled himself with the thought, "Well, nothing ventured, nothing gained." The following morning, he was somewhat surprised as seniors began to gravitate to his place of business and he heard them talking about yesterday and meeting this remarkable young boy or girl, of having their first ever chance to find out what was really going on in the lives of young people.

Word got out also at the high school, as you can well imagine, and on the following Thursday, over twice as many young people drifted into the flower shop, hoping for a rose or carnation to get them launched on a conversational adventure. They were disappointed when the florist said he would not be able to give them as many flowers that day. When they inquired why, he told them they might find this hard to believe, but about twenty minutes before, some seniors had come in looking for carnations and roses and had gone out walking up and down Main Street looking for teenagers.

Interesting! This breakdown of barriers occurred without new bylaws, complex strategic planning, or for that matter any complex social action planning. Nor had there been any blaring front-page stories or news headlines about a disconnect between Summerland adults and the teens who need them in their lives. All it took to begin to address a major community concern was for the young people and the seniors most vitally affected to find a way to get to know one another better.

And the changes did not end there. The seniors began to meet and talk with the kids and asked what they could do to make life better for them. They asked young people to come to one of their meetings and to tell them, among other things, what was the worst part of the week for them. The kids responded without hesitation: going to school on Monday morning.

The seniors were understandably baffled about how to respond, because they could not do much about school schedules.

But they worked on the problem and finally came up with what has been seen by many as one of the most innovative solutions to kids' Monday-morning school blues ever contrived. They went out and bought a dozen bright-red Elvis Presley vests, and for the next few years it was common to see three or four seniors standing at every entrance door to Summerland Secondary School early on Monday morning, personally greeting every student who walked into that school.

Summerland's seniors did not make their solution very complicated. They did not need to. They simply determined they would remember kids' names and they would remember something they said or something about them so that they could make a meaningful reconnection the following week. And connect they did! Soon seniors found themselves for the first time standing in line at a local convenience store not worrying about their safety, but instead actually conversing with somebody they already knew among the many young people standing in line with them.

This unusual community-building enterprise grew. When young people got to thinking of how much fun it was getting a chance every Monday morning to talk to seniors who cared about them, they went to the seniors and asked, "What's the hardest part of *your* life?" And the seniors answered without hesitation: "Computers, we hate them. If we could use them properly we would be able to keep in better touch with our families, our grandchildren, and our friends, but it's hard to learn something so new as you get older."

Armed with a better understanding of seniors' concerns, the kids came up with yet another first for Summerland. They talked to the seniors, to their school, to the local Internet provider. Impressed with their young people's innovative idea and resolve, the community rallied to provide renewed support to purchase and install computers in places where young people could teach basic computer skills to the people who cared enough to get up early every Monday morning to welcome them to school.

Variations of the Summerland model have been replicated in towns and cities throughout North America. More detailed information regarding the Summerland survey results and a more detailed description of the Summerland Asset Development Initiative can be found in their report published in early 2000 entitled *All Kids—Our Kids ... Asset Development Handbook*.

In the next chapter you will learn how other institutions and businesses have chosen to exploit technology—rather than relationship building—in response to a perceived lack of respect among young people.

LESSONS TO TAKE AWAY

1. In the late 1990s, the small town of Summerland, B.C., recognized that it had a problem: growing discord between the young people and seniors in the community.

2. In response, city council created the Summerland Asset Development Initiative and invited a renowned champion of youth to head up the fledgling youth movement.

3. After a comprehensive survey of youth, both seniors and young people responded in imaginative, simple, yet powerful ways to improve intergenerational relations.

Chapter 13

The Mosquito—
Technology Gone Mad

Only two things are infinite, the universe and
human stupidity, and I'm not sure about the former.
—ALBERT EINSTEIN

A COUPLE OF YEARS AGO, I received a short note from a friend and police officer who has spent much of his professional career finding and applying effective, respectful solutions to the challenges a small minority of youth represent in society today. He is focused on young people because he believes that effective prevention is the most promising approach to crime reduction. In his note he urged me to become familiar with what he had learned, to his dismay, was being touted as one major retailer's next line of defence in dealing with what was seen as an undesirable teen presence and behaviour in their stores. The retailer had found its answer through the application of a new technology.

Maybe you have never heard about Compound Security Systems' widely advertised, novel approach to the so-called youth problem. If you have teens in your family, a visit to the manufacturer's website may be edifying. Allow me to share briefly, from that website, a glimpse of what their revolutionary Mosquito™ has in store (pun intended) for your kids and mine.

> The Mosquito™ Anti Loitering Device / Anti-Vandal System … is the solution to the eternal problem of unwanted gather ings of youths and teenagers in shopping malls, around shops and anywhere else they are causing problems. The presence of these teenagers discourages genuine shoppers and custom-ers from coming into your shop, affecting your turnover and profits. Anti social behaviour has become the biggest threat to private property over the last decade and there has been no effective deterrent until now.
>
> Acclaimed by Police Forces of many areas of the United Kingdom, the Mosquito™ Security System has been described as "the most effective tool in our fight against anti social behaviour." Shopkeepers around the world have purchased the device to move unwanted gatherings of teenagers and anti social youths. Railway companies have placed the device to discourage youths from spraying graffiti on their trains and the walls of stations.

According to the manufacturer, "The Mosquito™ device emits a pulsed high frequency tone which disperses groups/individuals on the basis of annoyance/irritation." Ah, but not just any groups or individuals. This sonic "weapon" is an irritant only to those under the age of twenty-five.

As a promotional online "article" by JK Ellis reports ("Make Those Pesky Teenagers Run Away," ArticleSnatch.com):

> Compound Security Systems field trials have shown that teen-agers are acutely aware of the Mosquito and usually move away from the area within an average of 8–10 minutes. The system is completely harmless even with long term use. *The Times* newspaper in England reports that the device was first used at a Spar shop convenience store in Barry, South Wales, where

the owner Robert Gough was enthusiastic about the device's success in driving away the local youths. "Either someone has come along and wiped them off the face of the earth, or it's working" he is quoted as saying....

It seems that there is a very real medical phenomenon known as presbycusis or age related hearing loss which, according to *The Merck Manual of Diagnosis and Therapy*, "begins after the age of 20 but is usually significant only in persons over 65. It first affects the highest frequencies (18 to 20 kHz) notably in those who have turned 20 years of age."...

Is your business suffering from anti social youths driving your customers away or generally causing damage or nuisance?

Are you bothered by crowds of teenagers hanging around your street and making life unpleasant?

Mosquito ultrasonic deterrent can solve your problem.

I read the foregoing with total disbelief. Have we really plummeted to such a low level in our community problem-solving reservoir that we feel compelled to use technology to drive our kids out of places we have decided they should not be? With the purchasing power young people have today, they are among some of our most valuable customers. The fact is, retailers—and by extension, we as a society—need and want young people's money to help keep the economy going and, one must suppose, our profits climbing. We just don't *always* need and want them.

An Unenlightened and Discriminatory Response

Is this really the best solution society can come up with to respond to the isolated though, admittedly, unacceptable and disrespectful behaviour of a small percentage of young people? As parents, grandparents, and community leaders, is this the best way we can find to effectively respond to that small minority of teens whose behaviour we find annoying, anti-social, or repugnant?

More importantly, is this a message we want to deliver to the vast majority of our kids who do us proud every day? You see, the Mosquito is not very selective in terms of which kids receive its high-frequency "get lost" message.

I can only imagine how human rights lawyers will judge the notion of bombarding kids with what Canadian distributor Dynatrac Systems' corporate literature describes as a "hooligan repelling/high frequency sound that only the average thirteen to twenty-five-year-olds can hear." Who is next on the Mosquito manufacturer's agenda of potential targets? Does the company have a frequency that repels drunks on airplanes? Maybe one for the person who persists in driving their car or holding up a check-out line while they talk on their cellphone or send text messages ad nauseam?

How stupid! How sad! I shake my head that the Mosquito is being promoted and installed at a time when children's rights advocates worldwide are increasingly introducing positive app-roaches that focus on what the vast majority of our teens are doing right every day. Many young people are themselves increasingly involved in volunteering, getting an education, and serving as role models in their families, schools, neighbourhoods, and communi-ties. Yet we are being asked to support businesses that are going to zap our kids with the Mosquito. I don't think so! I hope not!

At least I am not the only one concerned about this new appli-cation of technology. The following passage is taken from a 2010 *Canadian Journal of Communication* article authored by Mitchell Akiyama of McGill University, entitled "Silent Alarm: The Mos-quito Youth Deterrent and the Politics of Frequency."

> Howard Stapleton, the inventor of the Mosquito, recently stated, "I never intended it to make kid-free zones but to com-bat anti-social behaviour and it should only be used where there is that" (quoted in "British Inventor of Teen-Repellent Device Wants Laws Regulating It," 2008). But the device does not target behaviour: it targets youth. Singling out individuals

rather than conduct, according to legal scholar Charlotte Walsh (2008), could be construed as criminal harassment. (p. 465)

Akiyama goes further, writing:

> In a social milieu that permits the use of the Mosquito, youth are not only devalued for their inability to "properly" participate in consumption, they are demonized for supposedly interfering with what are perceived to be its normally smooth workings. The Mosquito widens the gulf of understanding between generations, reinforcing an already deep sense of mutual suspicion and contempt. (p. 466)

As a parent and grandparent, I am outraged that this draconian, simplistic, and counter-productive corporate notion of the Mosquito could be introduced into my community, where the vast majority of teens deserve better from their elders. I am not a proponent of violence, but I can understand the frustration of seventeen-year-old Dodger Grace, who offered this online response after reading about the Mosquito technology. "It made me feel angry. I wanted to punch somebody in the face." His comment, no doubt offered in haste, obviously is not appropriate, but if we are going to help the Dodgers of this world to find a better way, we have to start talking to one another, not sending high-frequency sounds that only thirteen- to twenty-five-year-olds can hear.

Forewarned is indeed forearmed, so you may want to watch out for the Mosquito coming soon to a convenience store, shopping centre, or schoolyard near you and the teens in your life. Meanwhile, remember how the folks in Summerland met this challenge of inappropriate teen attitude and behaviour head-on a few years ago. They found a solution that did not involve instituting discriminatory technology and abusing the civil rights of young people. No, it was about bringing young people and the important adults in their community together, identifying challenges, and then joining forces to make sure adults and young people alike could live in an environment hallmarked by respect, tolerance, sharing, and, in the case of the Summerland kids, industry and self-sufficiency.

LESSONS TO TAKE AWAY

1. To combat teen loitering and vandalism, Compound Security Systems developed the Mosquito, a device that emits high-frequency sounds irritating to those under twenty-five.

2. The Mosquito not only discriminates against young people, it also targets all of them, regardless of their behaviour.

3. This technological "solution" is wrong, especially at a time when more and more police officers, educators, and parents are adopting positive approaches that focus on what teens are doing right.

Chapter 14

Ever Make a Mistake?
The Art of Apologizing

Have you ever wondered which hurts the most:
saying something and wishing you had not, or
saying nothing, and wishing you had?
—ANONYMOUS

MUCH OF THIS BOOK HAS FOCUSED on how and why kids benefit when significant adults in their lives take time to share their wisdom, experience, and values. This chapter offers encouragement to *parents* who find themselves in the midst of parental or family turmoil. In this chapter, you'll learn that even in times of inevitable creative tension between parents and teens, you can find something positive that can be injected into the conversation. Being fair and respectful can work magic when you are faced with inappropriate and unacceptable behaviour by young people.

This chapter's opening quotation speaks to my own parenting experience. Being a parent is a period of life that brings an inordinate amount of joy and satisfaction, an onslaught of tough questions and limitless uncertainty, accompanied by demands for occasional tough decision making. I used to think these challenges applied almost exclusively to the moms and dads who, like me, struggled to do the best they could for kids they would give their life for if the need arose. As I moved on in my parenting years, I came to understand that our young people face many of these same daily life issues, uncertainties, and challenges we do as parents, and if we can keep the lines of communication open, every waking day offers valuable teachable moments that can guide how they choose to behave.

Maybe an example will make this point clearer. Fourteen-year-old Audrey storms into the house after school and immediately announces her entire academic future is at risk if her mother does not drop everything she's doing and drive her back to school so she can retrieve a document necessary for completion of a project due tomorrow. Mom is in the midst of doing laundry, preparing supper, and helping Audrey's younger brother with his homework.

Here's a hypothetical "cool mom" response. You can create your own to fit your particular challenge and style.

"Welcome home, Audrey. I'm sorry to hear your homework was left at school and know you take pride in completing assignments on time. As you can see, I'm trying to do three or four things at once here, so we can eat on time and you can get to your practice tonight. I really need your help. You can choose to help your brother with his homework—you're better at math than I am—you can fold the laundry, or you can make a salad for supper. That will free up fifteen minutes of my time and I'll gladly take you back to school to get the missing homework before we eat supper. Which job would you like to help me with?"

Let's be honest. As parents, many of us enter this remarkable realm of raising children with high hopes, abounding energy, and maybe even a belief we can do as well as or better than our parents did. This kind of confidence is understandable and desirable. At the same time, most of us enter this period of our lives as realists, having seen enough of life and, more particularly, the vagaries of child rearing to understand that sometimes our family dynamics will fail to earn us the "Good Parenting" seal of approval. Sometimes things will go wrong for all parents. And we need to remind ourselves that things can go wrong as well for the kids in our lives, and they need our help in learning how to respond appropriately.

When we see our kids are struggling to find answers or resolution to challenges they face, what we say or do in reaction to their behaviour can range anywhere from being appropriate to hurtful, from being helpful to devastating. Thankfully, our kids are a resilient bunch and a simple apology and admission of our being wrong coupled with an occasional well-timed hug can move the relationship back to where we really wanted it to be in the first place. Of course, the same goes for kids. When in the heat of the moment they say or infer things that fall far short of the point they were trying to make, they need to learn, as we do, that a sincere apology can do wonders.

The opportunity to apologize might come when words spoken harshly or in anger are so personally hurtful, the message delivered seems irretrievable. When that happened between me and my sons and daughter, I well recall trying frantically to delete the undeletable—to take back what I wish I had never said in the first place. I learned from my kids that they sometimes felt that same sense of powerlessness when their spoken words had far exceeded the level of displeasure they felt toward their mom and me, a sibling, or even a friend.

Hurtful words can happen at times when our normal sound judgement and sense of fairness and proportion get skewed. Maybe all it takes is a badly timed bowl of spilled food to trigger our outburst, which, if the truth were told, had very little to do with cornflakes on the kitchen floor but a great deal to do with a rough day at the office, a parking ticket, or a bad night's sleep. When the errant bowl of cereal enters into this emotionally unstable atmosphere, the resulting blow-up often escalates far beyond the relatively harmless issue of spilled cereal; even the responsibility of the hapless "child offender" becomes moot.

The Messy Truth about Toothpaste

While you will get no magic pill here from me, here's a quick pre-emptive action you can take even before any of your potential family combatants reaches the accusing, faulting, shouting stage. It works best if you do this before you find yourself dealing with that Forrest Gump prediction, loosely interpreted here as "Stuff happens."

Sit down with the kids in your life and quietly share the simple truth, which, by the way, they already know. "Stuff" will sometimes happen. Tell them you want to talk with them about finding a way you can all prepare for it. I told my sons and daughter there would be times when we might find ourselves overreacting and saying unkind or unfair things that could be hurtful, unforgettable, and maybe unforgivable.

We talked about what it is like when you squeeze toothpaste out of a tube. We agreed it comes out easily, but if we unintentionally squeeze out too much, we will find it almost impossible to put the toothpaste back where it belongs. I told my children that unkind words spoken in a moment of anger or upset are much like toothpaste coming out of a tube. They come out very easily, but you can never quite get them back where they really belong.

Kids need to know there will be times in their life when they are upset with others, or other people will be upset with them, and inevitably the futile "It's his fault/her fault" argument will prevail. Here is your chance to take the high road and offer your kids some important advice.

"So from now on when I find myself having a disagreement with you," you could tell them, "I'll take the time to discuss our misunderstanding or disagreement and listen to your side of the story. If I'm in the wrong, I'll apologize. If we agree you're wrong, I'll welcome an apology from you. Now let's take a few minutes to find a better way of preventing a recurrence of something that hasn't been much fun for any of us."

While we're at it, here is one more nugget you may want to file away in your child behaviour emergency response kit. Once a disagreement or crisis has been resolved, take the time to exercise your right to have the final word as the adult in the relationship. Tell your kids that while you will not always like what they did, you will always still love them. Then, if you are up to it and circumstances allow, why not give them a hug or two? I'm the guy who has always appreciated and tried to act on a cardinal rule I once heard offered to parents: "Never be the first one to break a hug with your kids."

I recently received an e-mail from a father in response to my blog post referencing my belief that sometimes as parents we would do better with our kids if we adopted the silent approach, which epitomizes a good mime. This seems like an appropriate time, with his permission, to share that exchange with you.

> I must tell you I had a "bad DAD" moment last week. As soon as I did it, albeit obviously too late, I apologized. I guess it is all part of the process, we all make mistakes at times (both parents and kids) but it is important to recognize it and learn from it, but I should have been a Mime.

I responded:

> I had a quick chuckle over your "Bad Dad" moment. Not because they're funny or foreseeable, but because they are so easily recognized by those of us who have gone before you. We've all been there ... done it! It's a lousy feeling but welcome to the club. There is a high side though to us blundering our way through parenthood. When *we* make a mistake it can offer an important teachable moment for our kids.

What better opportunity to teach our kids how to apologize than an honest "David/Mary, there's something I need to talk to you about. Sometimes dads are wrong and this time I was wrong. I didn't listen or understand before blaming you for whatever did or didn't happen. You did the right thing by defending yourself and helping me understand your side of the story. I apologize for what I said. From now on, let's both agree to listen more carefully because in life there will always be differences, and while you and I may not always like what we say or do to each other ... I just want you to know I will always love you!"

In life, it is sometimes when we are at our worst that the greatest opportunities present themselves to teach our kids important lessons—in this case, apologizing and forgiving. Thanks for a great example of a dad doing it well!

For more on the challenges of parenting, including practical steps to improve parent-teen relations, read on to the next chapter.

LESSONS TO TAKE AWAY

1. As parents, our response to our children's behaviour can sometimes say more about us than it does about them.

2. By acknowledging we are far from perfect, we can invite discussion with our kids in advance about how we can respond to and recover from potentially hurtful emotional outbursts.

3. "Teachable moments" in parenting may come at times when our own behaviour is at its worst, so stay honest with your kids and always be quick to apologize.

Chapter 15

Stop the Parenting Bus ...
I Want to Get Off!

No matter how calmly you try to referee,
parenting will eventually produce bizarre behavior ...
—BILL COSBY

MAYBE YOU FEEL LIKE A FATHER I met one evening when I facilitated a Parents Together group, a mutual support/ self-help group for parents offered under the auspices of Boys and Girls Clubs of Greater Vancouver (now Boys and Girls Clubs of South Coast BC). Those groups comprised moms, dads, grandparents, and significant others who, by their own admission, were not having much fun raising teenagers. A single dad with three teens told his group, "Sometimes I feel like my primary purpose in life is to serve as a warning to other parents."

Ever felt that way? The feeling is like having an elephant sitting in the middle of the coffee table in your living room that nobody talks about. You just pretend it isn't really there. Parents dealing with disrespectful and rebellious kids often find themselves increasingly trapped in a slowly eroding support network. When you are in this situation, you do not have a lot of stories and successes that you really want to share with Grandma. Certainly not if your kids are skipping school, being disrespectful, smoking a variety of homegrown and imported vegetation, auditing and sampling your liquor cabinet, or pawning the family silver to cover the cost of entertainment. Maybe they are keeping your family continually on the ropes by running away or threatening to run away.

Life as a parent in these circumstances can get pretty lonely and isolating. A mom once told me the best thing that happened for her was when the local food store began 24-hour operations. This meant she could shop late rather have to face friends and neighbours who knew or *wanted* to know what her kids were up to. Parenting under these conditions can be discouraging, isolating, and frustrating; it can bring on an understandable sense of hopelessness. Some parents have told me *they* are the ones who want to run away from home. The danger, of course, is that you may come to believe you are the only person who is having this kind of experience with your kids. You may even have concluded there must be something wrong with you.

As I contemplated the pros and cons of including this chapter on some of the challenges of parenting, it occurred to me that I would have no shortage of raw material here. After all, as a father and grandfather, I find this somewhat familiar territory.

Let's start with a bias of mine. I think the phrase "troubled kids" may be the wrong term, because it implies that occasional inappropriate behaviour among teens is abnormal, something no "good" parent should have to anticipate or endure. A quick trip to the *Encarta Dictionary* dispels that notion. "Trouble *n:* a condition of distress, anxiety or danger." Yep, that is how I remember it felt when relationships in our family went sideways. And I did not think my wife and I had done that bad a job of parenting, although I recall times when our confidence and self-esteem were badly shaken by well-meaning friends or professionals who offered a magic pill solution or subtly implied that our kids' inappropriate behaviour was our fault.

A Commitment to Change

Around the time our kids were teens, I became aware of a book entitled *How to Deal With Your Acting-Up Teenager*, by Robert and Jean Bayard, both PhDs, based on the authors' experience raising five children as well as their experience as practising psychologists. Their approach became the foundation of Parents Together and similar mutual support groups that have offered encouragement, support, and practical ideas to concerned parents in Canada and the United States over the past thirty years. For many parents, reading this book helped them take their first tangible steps toward identifying, creating, and deploying constructive and respectful approaches aimed at turning things around in the parent-teen relationships that had brought concern and disruption to their lives. Terminology and issues have changed since this book was written thirty years ago, but to this day the principles offered by the Bayards remain applicable and valid.

Perhaps the simplest and most effective way for me to introduce you to the approach of the Parents Together program is to ask you to imagine yourself among a gathering of parents of acting-up teens who have come together for what can be an agonizing first meeting. Like them, you might be amazed as you look around the room and discover that everyone in the room looks so normal. Of course, that is because they are, but I have been told time and time again by parents of acting-up teens that they have come to believe they are less worthy, less normal, and that there must be something wrong with them.

Unresolved parent-teen conflict can lead to such feelings. It is a self-esteem-damaging and soul-destroying experience that is so insidious, you do not even realize you have fallen into the trap of believing that you are the one responsible for controlling your teen's behaviour.

So how you do you take the first steps toward turning things around? For starters, talk to a spouse or partner. If you are alone, seek out a trusted friend, neighbour, or relative and tell them you want to bring about a change in the relationship between you and your teenager. Tell your teen the same thing. Do this positively. Do not attach blame. Do not feel compelled to offer details. And anyway, you have not yet decided exactly how you are going to proceed. Just that you are! Tell yourself and anyone who will listen without judging that you will do whatever it takes to bring harmony, respect, and honesty back into the relationship between you and your teen.

To get the relationship back on track, you will need to accept the reality that as much as you may be tempted to try, you cannot change your teen's behaviour. You can only change the way in which you react to that behaviour. And when you do, your teen will feel compelled to alter their conduct. It can be a tricky concept and a difficult one to grasp in the midst of teen rebellion. But think about it. When was the last time someone else changed your behaviour?

Three Steps to Better Teen-Parent Relations

When I first considered including this chapter focusing on challenges many parents face, particularly in their kids' teen years, I was tempted to provide encouragement and practical ideas based on my memory of the Bayards' work and the Parents Together program. Then, in a moment of enlightenment, I had a better idea. I recalled the outstanding work of one Stephanie Carros, who served as program director of the Parents Together program out of Vancouver. I recalled as well the excellent resources she developed that underpinned the help offered to hundreds of parents who met in small groups once a week to resolve parent-teen conflict in their homes.

I spent a couple of hours with Stephanie, getting the advice of an expert in this field. With her permission and cooperation, what follows is a summary of what she told me, derived from her knowledge, her experience, and ideas contained in her handout entitled "Tools to Support Your Teen."

But first, some general guidelines of my own for this parenting journey.

- When making decisions affecting your teen, take time to engage them in establishing reasonable and fair limits. Kids need to learn how to make and apply rational decisions.

- Find ways to encourage and advance your teen's search for independence, consistent with their ability to handle it responsibly.

- Try to find at least one opportunity every day to honour and recognize your teen's goodness. It could be an achievement in school, sports, or music; kindness toward a brother or sister; a positive comment you heard about them from a neighbour or friend.

- Remain appropriately and vitally involved in their lives. Young people thrive on the interest and encouragement given sincerely by friends, parents, and important adults in their lives.

- Take time every day to tell them you love them. Don't make the assumption this is simply understood because you do. Say it!

Here is a three-step approach that has been adopted by untold numbers of parents trying to bring greater levels of respect, honesty, support, and fairness to their relationships with the young people in their lives. The three steps are as follows:

1   **Make a life list.**

2   **Divide the list.**

3   **Develop strategies.**

And here is a how-to description that can help you implement each step.

Step 1. Make a life list

Start by making a list of all of your teen's behaviours that bother you. Parents of the same teen need to each make their own list, because some of the behaviours that bother each of them will be different. Be specific—for example, saying "He's irresponsible" is too general. Instead, list the exact behaviours that led you to this statement. Here are a couple of examples of the kind of statements that will work better for you as you continue this exercise.

He abuses me verbally.

She skips school.

His hair is too long and bright red.

He refuses to do his homework.

She is late for school. most days

She stays out past curfew.

He smokes marijuana.

She smokes cigarettes in our house.

She will not do household chores.

He has no interest in anything but the Internet and his cellphone.

Step 2. Divide the list

Review your list and decide whether each "problem" behaviour belongs on your list or on your teen's. Divide a fresh sheet of paper into two columns. At the top of the left side, print the heading PARENT'S LIFE LIST. Place under that heading problems over which you have control and problems that affect your life directly.

Next, on the right side of the paper, print the heading TEEN'S LIFE LIST. Under this heading, place those problems over which you have *no control* or problems with consequences that affect *only your teen*. Identifying those problems can be tricky and challenging sometimes, because as parents, we sometimes erroneously come to believe we have complete control over everything our teenagers do. Apply the "do I or do I not?" test to realistically determine whether you have control over this behaviour.

Your two lists might look something like this:

PARENT'S LIFE LIST	TEEN'S LIFE LIST
Abuses me verbally.	Skips school.
Smokes cigarettes in our house.	Smokes marijuana.
Steals money from my wallet.	Refuses to do homework.
Will not do household chores.	Hair too long and bright red.

Okay, time to take a break, sit back, and have a cold, hard look at the two lists. At this point you may find you have been trying to control and accept responsibility for life list items that rightfully belong to your teenager. There is a good chance the parental list for which you can realistically accept responsibility will be shorter than you had previously thought.

When it is hard to decide, and it often is, which list a behaviour rightfully belongs on, here are a few guidelines that might help.

- It's possible you are trying to deal with more than one problem. Try breaking down the problem into smaller parts. For example, instead of "Rejects parental authority," write "Abuses car privileges."

- Break that down even further, for example: Returns car home later than agreed; Fails to replace gas used; Leaves garbage in car. (In fact, your teen may be a safe driver and you have no concerns there, so be specific about what the problem behaviours are.)

- Do not worry about whether or not you should be able to control a problem. The test to apply is, does it or does it not directly affect my life?

- Try to separate yourself from what you believe are society's expectations. Focus in on the difference between what generally affects your life or your teen's life. For example, society expects parents to make sure their teen does their homework. But whether or not they do their homework is beyond your control and only affects your teen.

- If the problem belongs to your TEEN'S LIFE LIST but you just cannot let go of it, ask yourself whether this is because your *worry* about it is the real problem. "Anxiety" is a significant issue for all of us as parents. If our fretting has become out-of-control, it does not matter whether the teen stops doing the behaviour that causes it. We will then just find something else to agonize over. It is our responsibility as parents to learn strategies to control our own anxieties.

- If you are having trouble allocating a behaviour to your teen's or your list, it may be because the problem belongs on *both* of your lists and will require a combination of strategies. Break down the problem into its smallest components and re-examine it to see if this is the case.

Step 3. Develop strategies

The third step in this teen-parent relationship-improvement plan is to develop strategies to deal with the problem behaviours you have identified and listed. This is the point when you begin to document practical and sometimes creative approaches you feel are fair, reasonable, and achievable in altering your teen's behaviour. Here's the process:

- *Transfer responsibility.* This is when you have determined that a problem rightfully belongs to your teen. The criteria? It doesn't affect you directly and you have no control over the outcome. Below you will find some approaches that have worked for others in turning over the responsibility.

- *Take a stand.* If the problem belongs to you, try not to lecture or moralize. You might find it helpful to practise with a friend or partner. At the risk of belabouring the point, this is where you get a chance to practise your "I" statements. Set aside the temptation to blame (more step-by-step guidelines follow).

- *Avoid triggers* that may not have worked in the past. "Where do you find your loser friends?" "You're just like ... so-and-so." "You'll never get a job with hair like that!"

- *Talk with others*—parents, professionals, and school counsellors—for support.

- *Attend to self-care.* It's particularly important for all parents to take the time to look after themselves. If we don't, then we can hardly expect our teenagers to learn from our example.

As you work your way through making your list, dividing the list, and developing strategies, be aware that there is an additional category of problems that occasionally arise. These are major issues such as depression, attempted suicide, addiction, mental health and major physical health issues. These are problems so serious that while your parental involvement continues to be critically important, you must move that involvement to a different level. If you have witnessed these changes in the behaviour of your son or daughter or even suspect one of these problems is an underlying factor, it is time to immediately seek professional help.

1. **Get information and seek resources.**

2. **Get help for your teen.**

3. **Create a support network.**

4. **Take care of yourself and your own needs.**

5. **Make a plan and follow it through.**

How to Turn Over Responsibility

Turning over responsibility for a problem that belongs to your teen does not mean withdrawing interest, caring, or support or disengaging from your teen's life. Rather, it is a proactive way to solve problems that shows respect for your teen's ability to make his or her own decisions. What we believe tends to be self-fulfilling, so trust that your teen is capable of making decisions over things that he or she can control and that affect his or her life. Believe that your teens will learn as much from their mistakes as from their successes, as long as they are allowed to experience the consequences of their decisions

Here is a step-by-step approach that will help you walk through the process of turning responsibility over to your teen.

- *Pick an item* from your teen's life list that you believe you can transfer responsibility on without too much difficulty.

- *Detach* yourself as much as possible from the process— watch your teen's behaviour and reactions as an interested and curious observer.

- *Relax* by taking deep breaths and being calm. Our body language and tone of voice are important translators through which our messages to the significant people in our lives, and particularly to our teens, are communicated.

- *Rehearse* what you want to say, using words that are comfortable for you. Test out your approaches with a partner or trusted friend.

- *Use the five-part process* that follows to transfer responsibility to your teen for the particular behaviour you have identified.

1   State your feelings and thoughts.

2   Recognize your teen's feelings.

3   Turn over the responsibility.

4   Show trust.

5   Address your part of the problem, offer support, and
    state your boundaries.

Here is one example to illustrate how the process works. Let's assume your teen is not doing their homework.

1   **State your feelings and thoughts.** I'm sick and tired of trying to get you do your homework. Nothing I have done has worked.

2   **Recognize your teen's feelings.** I don't believe my constant nagging has been much fun for you either.

3   **Turn over the responsibility.** From now on, I am not going to be harping at you about your homework.

4   **Show trust.** I know you are capable of making decisions about your education and future that are right for you.

5   **Address your part of the problem, offer support, and state your boundaries.** From now on, I will not be discussing your homework with you. If you would like some help, please let me know before 9:00 P.M.

Here is another example of one parent's use of the five-step process in turning over responsibility to a teen known to be smoking marijuana. Keep in mind there is no one right way to transfer responsibility, and any approach you use must fit you, your teenager, and the life experience and values you share As a prelude to the five steps, it's often helpful if you name the specific problem, for example, "I hear from your teachers and friends that you are smoking marijuana."

1   **State your feelings and thoughts.** I worry about your health and how this behaviour will affect your school grades.

2   **Recognize your teen's feelings.** I know you think I'm old-fashioned and you think marijuana is safe and harmless.

3   **Turn over responsibility.** From now on, I am not going to hassle you about your marijuana use. This is your life and your body.

4   **Show trust.** Know you're capable of doing your own research about the effects of marijuana and trust you will do what is right for you.

5   **Address your part of the problem, offer support, and state your boundaries.** For my part, I will not allow marijuana in this house and will confiscate any I find. If you need help from me, please ask.

You can use this five-step process to address items on the TEEN'S LIFE LIST. To reiterate, start with the less contentious issues, and address them one at a time. You may find that the process gets easier each time, and you may notice positive changes in your teen's behaviour as a result of your actions. You should definitely experience less conflict in your relationship. But that still leaves the items on the PARENT'S LIFE LIST.

Taking a Stand on Items on the Parent's Life List

This is where you can begin to address parent-teen issues that you have thoughtfully concluded are affecting you directly and over which you have some ability to bring resolution. Whoever said

"Rome wasn't built in a day" must have parented teens. Carefully select one issue at a time. There's much to be said for taking on one you feel most confident can be resolved. Teens need time to adjust to your new approach and, like you, they will do better building on success. Here's one approach you can use to work through these problem behaviours.

First, state the problem and negotiate a fair deal. "I find you are spending too much time on the Internet and on your cellphone, and I want the amount of time to decrease. I want to try to work out something together. I think your computer, iPod, and cellphone should be turned off during meals and on weeknights by 8:00 p.m. Does that sound fair to you?" After an agreement has been reached, take the time to summarize your understanding. If the teen does not contribute, make your own deal.

Give your teen a few days to remember and abide by the agreement. Once you have an agreement, if your teen is not honouring that agreement, it's time to insist with persistence. "It's past 8:00 p.m. I need you to turn off your cellphone and your computer right away! I know you would like to finish your phone call, but I need you to turn it off." You may find yourself repeating this last statement many times. After you have done so, withdraw from the conversation, knowing you have stuck up for your rights.

If the agreement is not honoured, that is, your teen does not shut off their technology at the agreed time, say what you will do if the task is not completed. "If you do not honour our agreement, I will remove your computer from your bedroom and discontinue payment of your cellphone plan." Say this calmly and follow through as soon as possible.

At this point you may find it necessary to remind yourself you are travelling in uncharted waters. There are no easy and magic answers. Parenting teens, like most of life's most important journeys, requires honesty, patience, respect, negotiation, and mutual caring and understanding from both parties.

For reasons of space, I have offered the bare essentials needed to start you thinking and maybe get you started. Remember, above all, to look after yourself. Most parents of acting-up teens forgo any self-care to devote all of their energy to reacting to their teen's behaviour. If you and I do not treat ourselves with respect, we can hardly expect others to do so. When we are feeling good and healthy, we are better able to be role models for our teens and, not surprisingly, we parent better.

And don't feel you have to embark on this enhanced parenting adventure without support. Where was it ever written that parents were placed on this earth to raise kids in isolation, that it is a sign of weakness for moms and dads to seek advice and support from others? Do seek help from others and be encouraged and take heart from the following. Statistics tell us that most of these kids are going to do just fine, so every morning when you get up to prepare for another day, take a minute to stand in front of a mirror and say to yourself with conviction, "I'm doing the best job that I can, and it should be enough for any kid to grow up on!"

Of necessity, this chapter has dealt with what for many of us is the unforeseen and sometimes discouraging part of raising healthy kids. But after all, if it seems broken, we ought to try to fix it. In the next chapter, you will have a chance to reflect on the joys that can only come to those of us privileged to share in this wonderful experience called parenting. You will be reminded of a hundred ways you and the children in your life are learning, laughing, growing, and sharing as you journey together in the remarkable phenomenon called family.

LESSONS TO TAKE AWAY

1. Parenting acting-up teens can be a discouraging, isolating, and frustrating experience. Realize that you are not alone and reach out to others for help.

2. An important part of addressing teen-parent conflict is to recognize that you cannot change your teen's behaviour. You can only change the way you react to that behaviour.

3. Parents Together takes a three-step approach to restoring respect, honesty, support, and fairness to parent-teen relations: Take time to identify the challenges you face. Learn how to back off on issues beyond your control and to take a stand on those affecting you directly and within your power to change. Above all, take time to care for yourself. You and your teens need and deserve that.

Chapter 16

Lessons My Children and Grandchildren Taught Me

Be the kind of person you
always wanted your parents to be.
—ANONYMOUS

FAITHFUL READER: If you have made it this far, you may recall I dedicated this book to my wife, Maureen, my sons, daughter, and four grandchildren, who have been such an important part of my life. In closing, here is a sampling of some approaches or activities they have told me are important to them. Most are simple ways to show interest and support that I work hard to remember and practise every day.

Every one of us can have a list like this. While we seldom put these simple practices to paper, you may want to take a few minutes to inventory the things you already do naturally and well that benefit young people. It is my guess you will be pleasantly surprised when you are reminded how you already support and encourage kids in a casual way. You may find you would like to add a few new ideas to your personal repertoire and then intentionally introduce one or more of them daily in the lives of young people you influence. My own list, which follows, acquired over many years, may remind you of important things you already do. In addition, it may trigger some amazing new approaches with potential to bring satisfaction to you and the young people in your life.

1. Remember their friends' names.

2. Share their worries.

3. Listen to and hear their stories.

4. Tell them you love them.

5. Teach them by example.

6. Apologize when you're wrong.

7. Play games with them.

8. Be a gracious winner or loser.

9. Introduce them to the magic of doing something for somebody else.

10. Teach honesty by being honest.

11. Recognize and honour their achievements.

12. Celebrate their uniqueness.

13. Share their disappointments.

14. Teach respect by respecting them.

15. Learn to listen; listen to learn.

16. Set fair and consistent boundaries.

17. Play make-believe.

18. Encourage racial tolerance through your actions.

19. Ask for their opinions and advice.

20. Marvel at their accomplishments.

21. Focus on their potential, not on their limitations.

22. Be courteous to them (and in their presence).

23. Supportively, help them to debrief their mistakes.

24. Laugh together ... a lot!

25. Say please and thank you.

26. Cherish sunrises together.

27. Always keep your promises.

28. Act your age, but never lose sight of the child within you.

29. Skip stones across the water.

30. Focus on their kindness.

31. Look into their eyes when you talk to them.

32. Surprise them.

33. Let them surprise you.

34. Write encouraging chalk messages on their driveways.

35. Teach them to love and respect animals.

36. Smile when you greet them.

37. Bake and burn cookies together.

38. Sit quietly or tell stories around a campfire together.

39. Introduce them to people they want to meet.

40. Walk together barefoot in the sand.

41. Ask them to help plan the time you spend together.

42. Build sandcastles together; take pictures of your creations.

43. Together, plan a "bring a friend" day or activity.

44. Burn marshmallows together.

45. Believe in them.

46. Together, find the child in both of you.

47. Show trust: let them cover you in sand.

48. Be amazed by their stories.

49. Cheer at their games.

50. Dream together.

51. Validate their value.

52. Send them encouraging texts or e-mails.

53. Together, watch in awe the setting sun.

54. Count satellites together.

55. Laugh at the rain and snow.

56. Get wet … be silly … have fun!

57. Build a snowman together.

58. Search for four-leaf clovers.

59. Say no and mean it.

60. Say yes and follow through.

61. Make up stories where they are the heroes or heroines.

62. Keep them safe.

63. Take them fishing; put the worm on the hook.

64. Respect them no matter what.

65. Sing together.

66. Help them with their homework; let them help you with yours.

67. Fly and crash kites together.

68. Substitute TV time with adventure together time.

69. Empower them to be their best.

70. Catch them doing something they would want to be caught doing.

71. Hold hands as you gaze in wonder at the moon.

72. Praise their preciousness.

73. Value their opinions.

74. Hold their hand when it matters.

75. Make snow angels together.

76. Listen to their music.

77. Cry together if it seems right.

78. Expect their best—not perfection.

79. Tell them how lucky you are to have them.

80. Play hopscotch together.

81. Focus on what matters to them, not on what's the matter with them.

82. Be happy, be kind, be enthusiastic, be responsible. Simply be a good role model.

83. Tell them when they're wrong and then help them find a better way.

84. When you've disagreed, tell them you will still always love them.

85. Comfort them when they are frightened.

86. Volunteer together.

87. Listen more … talk less.

88. Celebrate admirable or responsible behaviour.

89. Teach them the gift of giving.

90. Love them as if they are irreplaceable—they are!

91. Solve problems together.

92. Read to them; ask them to read to you.

93. Play "I spy" with them.

94. Be the last to break a hug.

95. Hang their artwork on your fridge door.

96. Offer options and help them choose the best for them.

97. Laugh over spilled milk.

98. Remind yourself to choose your battles carefully.

99. Remember, what we seek from our children, we must first of all give them.

100. Never, never, never give up on them!

Conclusion

Action speaks louder than words but not nearly as often.
—MARK TWAIN

MOST OF US UNDERSTAND THERE ARE no quick fixes to societal issues that face the children and youth living within our influence today. We recognize that only by working together will we effectively address the challenges of the kind of modern world we wish live in. And, as this book has tried to show, there is growing evidence that children and young people today are more inclined than ever before toward being actively engaged in changing the world for the better. They are raising money and resources for developing countries, volunteering their time with seniors and younger children, engaging in peer counselling, and spending vacations building homes and schools for kids less fortunate than they are.

My concluding hope is that good people who read this book will first recognize, then intentionally increase the important positive influence they have in the lives of young people. Maybe they will focus a little less on the negatives and instead increasingly focus on the strengths and gifts that both adults and young people can bring to bear in solving the most challenging and complex of our world's problems. Together we will be most successful when we start catching the majority of kids and the adults in their lives doing something right, rather than dwelling on a minority of highly profiled negative behaviours that too often draw the attention of modern media.

It will be important to remind ourselves occasionally that the best chance for our children and young people to achieve and exceed their potential does not lie in more government intervention, in new and more restrictive laws and bylaws, in massive injections of money, or in the creation of expensive programs. As it was for each of us, so it will be for the children within our influence. Healthy child development happens in the presence of those significant and compelling people in our lives who take the time to teach by example important lessons such as honesty, compassion, tolerance, respect, industry, and enthusiasm.

This book was written for those of you who understandably wonder if and where the solutions lie, who wonder what your role could possibly be and how in a practical way you can get involved daily and make a difference in the lives of young people. I hope you will have found some of the answers and inspiration you seek: in the stories of James Michener and the garbage man; Teddy, his teacher Mrs. Thompson, and the rhinestone bracelet; the physical education teacher who altered my life in only a few minutes; the remarkable seniors and teens of Summerland; and the Penticton high school where nobody fails.

I will leave you with two rhetorical questions that offer a fitting closing challenge for all of us:

If not now, then when?

If not you, then who?

Appendix

FAST FACTS ABOUT DEVELOPMENTAL ASSETS FOR YOUNG PEOPLE*

Immunizations keep young children healthy and protect them from disease. Similarly, Developmental Assets help kids make healthy choices and inoculate them against a wide range of risk-taking behaviours, including substance abuse, violence, and school failure. The more assets young people have, the more likely they are to be healthy.

Most young people surveyed by Search Institute have at least some assets (83 percent say they have 11 or more). But having only some of the assets is like getting only some of your shots. You might be protected against measles, but you could still get polio or hepatitis. That's why it's important to focus on giving young people all of the assets they need to be healthy.

- **Young people with more assets are less likely to engage in risk-taking behaviours.** Young people with 10 or fewer assets say they are involved in an average of about 3.8 high-risk behaviours. Young people with 31 assets or more report an average of less than 1 high-risk behaviour.

- **As young people's assets increase,** their positive behaviours also increase. While young people with 10 or fewer assets report an average of 2.6 positive behaviours, those with 31 assets or more average 6.2 positive behaviours. This includes succeeding in school, helping others, valuing diversity, and exhibiting leadership.

- **The average young person surveyed has 20 of the 40 assets.** But levels of assets decrease for older youth. While the average student in Grade 6 surveyed has 22.7 assets, the average student in Grade 12 surveyed has 19 assets.

- **The most common is asset 40: Positive view of personal future.** Seventy-five percent of young people surveyed report having this asset.

- **The least common is asset 17: Creative activities.** Only 20 percent of young people report having this asset.

- **Girls, on average, have more assets than boys.** However, boys are more likely to have assets 10: Safety; 38: Self-esteem; and 39: Sense of purpose.

- **Most assets decrease in frequency between Grades 6 and 12.** The assets that decrease the most are 12: School boundaries (74 percent vs. 44 percent); 15: Positive peer influence (87 percent vs. 50 percent); and 31: Restraint (73 percent of Grade 6 students vs. 21 percent of Grade 12 students).

- **Assets that increase in frequency between Grades 6 and 12 are** 10: Safety (41 percent vs. 68 percent); 23: Homework (33 percent vs. 50 percent); and 37: Personal power (39 percent vs. 54 percent).

* Based on data from the *Search Institute Profiles of Student Life: Attitudes and Behaviors Survey;* gathered in 2010 from almost 90,000 students in Grades 6 to 12 (ages approximately 11 to 18) from 111 communities in 26 U.S. states.

Permissions

The article by Patrice Releford on pages 38–39 originally appeared in the *Minneapolis Star Tribune*. It is reprinted with the newspaper's permission.

The list of 40 Developmental Assets™ in chapter 5 is reprinted with permission. Copyright © 1997, 2006 Search Institute. All rights reserved. No other use is permitted without prior permission from Search Institute, 615 First Avenue NE, Minneapolis, MN 55413; www.search-institute.org.

The graphs and pie chart on pages 46, 47 and 51, the list of frequently asked questions on pages 48–51, and the "Fast Facts" in the appendix are reprinted with permission from *Pass It On! Ready to Use Handouts for Asset Builders*, Handouts 2, 4, and 3, respectively. Copyright © 1999, 2006 Search Institute®, Minneapolis, MN; www.search-institute.org. All rights reserved.

The illustration on page 75 is reprinted with permission from Simon Sinek's book *Start with Why: How Great Leaders Inspire Everyone to Take Action* (Portfolio Trade, 2011).

Some of the material in chapter 15 on the Parents Together program was provided by and is used with the permission of Stephanie Carros.

References and Resources

Books, Articles, and Reports

Akiyama, Mitchell. "Silent Alarm: The Mosquito Youth Deterrent and the Politics of Frequency." *Canadian Journal of Communication* 35 (2010): 455–71.

Bayard, Robert T., and Jean Bayard. *How to Deal With Your Acting-Up Teenager: Practical Advice for Desperate Parents.* M. Evans & Company, 1986. Also available in 1998 edition.

Benson, Peter L. *All Kids Are Our Kids: What Communities Must Do to Raise Caring and Responsible Children and Adolescents.* 2nd ed. Jossey-Bass, 2006.

Benson, Peter L., Judy Galbraith, and Pamela Espeland. *What Kids Need to Succeed: Proven, Practical Ways to Raise Good Kids.* 3rd ed. Free Spirit Publishing, 2012.

Clapham, Ward. *Breaking with the Law: The Story of Positive Tickets.* Ward Clapham, 2010.

District of Summerland. *All Kids—Our Kids ... Asset Development Handbook.* Summerland, BC, 2000.

Dynatrac Systems Canada Inc. "Retailers Fighting Back Against Teen Loitering" [press release]. July 31, 2007. http://www.marketwire.com/press-release/dynatrac-systems-canada-inc-retailers-fighting-back-against-teen-loitering-756034.htm

Ellis, JK. "Make Those Pesky Teenagers Run Away." ArticleSnatch.com. http://www.articlesnatch.com/Article/Make-Those-Pesky-Teenagers-Run-Away/295783

Helping Kids Succeed—Alaskan Style. Youth Developmental Assets Framework, 2002.

Hondro, Marcus. "Divorce Rate 40% in Canada as Vanier Inst. Releases Family Report." *Suite101.com,* October 4, 2010.

Moscovitch, Arlene. *Good Servant, Bad Master? Electronic Media and the Family.* Contemporary Family Trends. Ottawa, ON: Vanier Institute of the Family, 2007.

Pattinson, Keith. "Healthy Communities … Healthy Youth." *Family Connections,* Winter 1998.

Search Institute. *Developmental Assets: A Profile of the Youth of Summerland—Attitudes and Behaviours.* Report commissioned by the Summerland Asset Development Initiative. Minneapolis, MN: Search Institute, 1999.

Sinek, Simon. *Start with Why: How Great Leaders Inspire Everyone to Take Action.* Portfolio Trade, 2011.

Vanier Institute of the Family. *Families Count: Profiling Canada's Families IV.* 2010. http://www.vanierinstitute.ca/families_ count_-_profiling_canadas_families_iv

———. "Four in Ten Marriages End in Divorce." *Fascinating Families,* issue 41, October 26, 2011.

Websites

Big Brothers Big Sisters of Victoria and Area.
www.bbbsvictoria.com

Boys and Girls Clubs of South Coast BC. www.bgc-gv.bc.ca

City of St. Albert. "Assets at Work."
www.stalbert.ca/assets-at-work

Compound Security Systems. "Mosquito Security Devices."
www.compoundsecurity.co.uk/security-information/
mosquito-devices

Every Kid in Our Communities of Leeds & Grenville.
www.everykid.on.ca

Free the Children. www.freethechildren.com

Lions Quest Canada. The Centre for Positive Youth
Development. www.lionsquest.ca

Parents Together. Boys and Girls Clubs of South Coast BC.
www.bgc-gv.bc.ca/content.asp?DocID=106. Look for the
group in your area.

Positive Tickets. www.positivetickets.com

Q'wemtsín Health Society. www.Qwemtsin.org

Ryan's Well Foundation. www.ryanswell.ca

Safe Communities Canada. www.safecommunities.ca

Search Institute. www.search-institute.org

Secwepemc Cultural Education Society. www.secwepemc.org

Vanier Institute of the Family. www.vanierinstitute.ca

Index

About the Author

KEITH PATTINSON is a professional speaker and youth advocate who has worked with young people and their families most of his life. He began his career as a teen volunteer when he co-founded the Boys and Girls Club of Kamloops, B.C. He later worked with Boys and Girls Clubs locally, provincially, and nationally in Vancouver, Montreal, and Calgary. Keith went on to introduce Boys and Girls Clubs in more than twenty towns and cities across Canada.

Keith has helped to spearhead many innovative services and approaches. In 1980, he co-founded Mountain Plains Community Services, an agency offering community-based residential services to troubled kids throughout the province of Alberta. He was instrumental in developing the Enviros Wilderness School for young offenders in Alberta, the Parents Together program across B.C., and the Vancouver-based Odyssey Substance Abuse program.

Not a retiring kind of guy, in 2001 Keith launched Keith Pattinson & Friends, offering keynotes and training that focus on positive youth development and engagement, practical strength-based strategies, and Search Institute's Asset Approach. His thoughtful, engaging, and often funny presentations focus on the audience's potential to change young lives for the better.

In his presentations and in this book, Keith offers hope, encouragement, and practical ideas to those who wish to become increasingly significant influences in the lives of young people. He shares his wisdom with groups that include students, parents, educators, and police officers. In hundreds of workshop evaluations, he has been described as one of Canada's most inspirational, humorous, and dynamic communicators.

Keith and his wife live in Delta, B.C. They have three children and four grandchildren.

Recipient of the following awards

- **Caring Canadian Award,** from the Governor General of Canada, which recognizes individuals who volunteer their time and efforts to help their fellow citizens —*July 2012*

- **Friend of Youth Award,** from the Boys and Girls Clubs of Greater Vancouver, in recognition of a lifetime of improving the quality of life for young people and families throughout British Columbia—*June 2003*

- **Paul Harris Fellow,** by Rotary International of Chicago, Illinois, acknowledging his lifetime of outstanding service to children, youth, families, and communities—*November 2001*

- **Anthony J. Hume Award of Distinction,** from the B.C. Ministry of Public Safety and Solicitor General, in recognition of his outstanding contribution toward crime prevention and community safety—*October 2001*

- **Boys and Girls Clubs of Canada Silver Keystone Award,** honouring his role across Canada as an innovator, leader, role model, and passionate champion of children and families—*February 1982*

Author Keith Pattinson with His Excellency the Right Honourable David Johnston, Governor General of Canada, at his presentation of the Governor General's Caring Canadian Award, July 2012, Victoria, British Columbia. The Caring Canadian Award recognizes individuals who volunteer their time and efforts to help their fellow citizens. The award also brings to light the example set by these unsung heroes and the positive impact they have in their communities.

Photo: Sgt Ronald Duchesne, Rideau Hall. © Her Majesty the Queen in Right of Canada represented by the Office of the Secretary to the Governor General (2012). Reproduced with the permission of the Office of the Secretary to the Governor General.

A Master Storyteller Shares His Wisdom

Keith Pattinson has been acknowledged by hundreds of Canadian audiences as a master storyteller whose message offers hope, encouragement, and practical ideas to those who wish to become increasingly significant influences in the lives of young people.

Keynotes—30 Minutes to 1 Hour

Popular for events such as staff or volunteer recognition, agency annual meetings or anniversary events, professional conferences, and training days. Topics include:

- Giving Our Kids What They Need to Succeed in Life
- What Are the 40 Developmental Assets?
- Kids Can Be Asset Builders Too

Workshops and Seminars—2 Hours to 2 Days

These events can be customized to meet the needs of a wide range of audiences, including parents, police officers, children and teens, childcare workers, teachers, probation officers, grandparents and senior citizens, service clubs, local/provincial/national youth and family conference attendees, and youth and family service providers. Types of events offered include:

- Developmental Assets workshops
- Parenting workshops
- Police officer trainings
- School assemblies or workshops
- Youth leadership training

Each workshop is designed to meet the needs of its audience. Whenever possible, these workshops offer the opportunity for interactive learning about ideas that can be applied by each and every person when they leave the presentation.

To learn more, visit **www.keithpattinson.com**

- Book Keith as a speaker or workshop leader
- Create a customized seminar for your group
- Purchase bulk copies of this book at a discount

Contact Keith at kpattinson@dccnet.com

Follow Keith:
on Twitter @talkaboutkids

on Facebook facebook

Feedback from parents

"I needed to be reminded of my kids' assets…. The presentation made me really want to go home and hug my kids."

"Incredible presentation. Brought tears to my eyes…. Has made me think about what I can do right away to build stronger relationships with any youth."

"Made me realize that my child's significant relationships with other family members are an important and meaningful asset to my son's growth and development."

"Opened my eyes to how much children really need us as positive role models in their lives."

Feedback from teachers, police officers, and youth workers

"Your stories were very inspiring and very relevant to my personal and professional life. The concept of asset building will alter forever the way in which I connect positively with all young people."

"I'd lost sight of the importance of instilling positive attributes in my students…. I feel encouraged and confident to work at 'catching my students doing something right.'"

"I feel renewed in my effort to nurture the children and youth I work with and those I encounter for only a brief time."

"As a school liaison officer, I end up spending an hour or two at a time with a kid in crisis, at least once a week.... You reminded me how much that hour or two might mean to that one person."

"Now I have concrete ideas on how I can make a difference—in my community, at work, and with people I see and meet."

Feedback from teens

"It's not easy to get my full attention in class, but you are an inspiring speaker and you did."

—RICKY, 15 YEARS

"Helped me to realize what it takes for a child to do well in their life and in the world.... Thanks to you I now know the reason why some kids grow up with ease and others struggle."

—LISA, 16 YEARS

"Communities need highly concerned people to take charge in empowering youth. Perhaps talking more about these assets will urge others to change their attitudes."

—ANDREA, 16 YEARS

"Sounds so simple, but how truly powerful. I will hold onto your stories for a long time.... It's a good feeling to know that there are some adults that care what happens to the youth and don't just give up on us."

—CHRISTINE, 15 YEARS